Ancient Civilizations

HARCOURT BRACE SOCIAL STUDIES

ACTIVITY BOOK

Teacher's Edition

HARCOURT BRACE & COMPANY

Orlando Atlanta Austin Boston San Francisco Chicago Dallas
New York Toronto London

Visit The Learning Site at http://www.hbschool.com

Copyright © by Harcourt Brace & Company

All rights reserved. No part of this publication may be reproduced or transmitted in any form or by any means, electronic or mechanical, including photocopy, recording, or any information storage and retrieval system, without permission in writing from the publisher.

Requests for permission to make copies of any part of the work should be mailed to the following address: School Permissions, Harcourt Brace & Company, 6277 Sea Harbor Drive, Orlando, Florida 32887-6777.

HARCOURT BRACE and Quill Design is a registered trademark of Harcourt Brace & Company.

For permission to reprint copyrighted material, grateful acknowledgment is made to the following sources:

Doubleday, a division of Bantam Doubleday Dell Publishing Group, Inc.: From *Alexander of Macedon: The Journey to World's End* by Harold Lamb. Text copyright 1946 by Harold Lamb.

Zondervan Publishing House: Scripture from the *New Revised Standard Version Bible.* Text copyright 1989 by the Division of Christian Education of the National Council of the Churches of Christ in the U.S.A.

Printed in the United States of America

ISBN 0-15-310313-2

2 3 4 5 6 7 8 9 10 073 01 00 99

The activities in this book reinforce or extend social studies concepts and skills in **ANCIENT CIVILIZATIONS**. There is one activity for each lesson and skill. Reproductions of the activity pages appear with answers in the Teacher's Edition.

CONTENTS

UNIT 1

Chapter 1

Lesson 1	What's in a Word?	1
Lesson 2	How Old Is That Fossil?	2
Skill	How to Use Latitude and Longitude	3
Lesson 3	Early Agriculture Around the World	4
Skill	How to Read a Parallel Time Line	5–6
Lesson 4	A Picture of Daily Life	7
Skill	How to Formulate a Generalization	8
Chapter Review	People of the Stone Age	9

Chapter 2

Lesson 1	The Importance of Resources	10–11
Lesson 2	Sumerian Culture	12
Lesson 3	The Code of Hammurabi	13–14
Skill	How to Compare Maps with Different Projections	15–16
Lesson 4	King Solomon's Trade Agreement	17–18
Lesson 5	A Time Line of Money	19
Skill	How to Compare Information with Graphs	20–21
Chapter Review	Southwest Asia	22

UNIT 2

Chapter 3

Lesson 1	Egypt and the Nile	23
Lesson 2	The Gods of Ancient Egypt	24
Lesson 3	More About Pyramids	25–26
Skill	How to Solve a Problem	27
Lesson 4	In Memory of King Tutankhamen	28–29
Lesson 5	The Pharaoh Queen	30
Skill	How to Follow Routes on a Map	31
Chapter Review	Ancient Egypt	32

Chapter 4

Lesson 1	The People of Nubia	33
Lesson 2	More About Kush	34–35
Skill	How to Use a Historical Map	36
Chapter Review	Ancient Nubia	37

UNIT 3

Chapter 5

Lesson 1	Rivers of India	38–39
Lesson 2	Life in the City	40
Lesson 3	A Family of Languages	41
Skill	How to Use a Cultural Map	42
Lesson 4	The Influence of Ashoka	43
Lesson 5	Military Technology	44–45
Chapter Review	India and Persia	46

Chapter 6

Lesson 1	Climate of China	47–48
Lesson 2	In the Beginning	49
Skill	How to Use Elevation Maps	50–51
Lesson 3	Confucius Said . . .	52–53
Skill	How to Identify Causes and Their Effects	54–55
Lesson 4	A China Diary	56–57
Lesson 5	Ancient Chinese Soldiers	58
Lesson 6	The Han Heritage	59
Skill	How to Classify Information	60
Chapter Review	China	61

UNIT 4

Chapter 7

Lesson 1	A Nation of Islands, Peninsulas, & Water	62
Lesson 2	Ancient Palaces of Crete	63
Skill	How to Compare Different Kinds of Maps	64–65
Lesson 3	Using Greek Root Words	66
Lesson 4	What's Holding It Up?	67
Skill	How to Predict Likely Outcomes	68
Lesson 5	Alexander the Great Learns to Sword-Fight	69–70
Chapter Review	Ancient Greece	71

Chapter 8

Lesson 1	Geography of Italy	72
Lesson 2	Roman Government	73
Skill	How to Make a Thoughtful Decision	74
Lesson 3	The Roman Empire	75
Skill	How to Compare Historical Maps	76
Lesson 4	Roman Military Might	77
Lesson 5	Christianity Today	78
Skill	How to Read a Telescoping Time Line	79–80
Lesson 6	The Germanic Tribes	81
Chapter Review	Ancient Rome	82

UNIT 5

Chapter 9

Lesson 1	Finding Places in South America	83–84
Lesson 2	Olmec Accomplishments	85
Skill	How to Learn from Artifacts	86
Lesson 3	Mayan Math	87
Skill	How to Use a Double-Bar Graph	88
Chapter Review	The Olmecs and the Mayas	89

Chapter 10

Lesson 1	The Aztecs	90
Skill	How to Compare Maps with Different Scales	91
Lesson 2	To Market, To Market Aztec Style	92
Lesson 3	Inca Record Keeping	93
Skill	How to Evaluate Information and Sources	94
Chapter Review	The Aztecs and the Incas	95

UNIT 6

Chapter 11

Lesson 1	Europe Today	96–97
Skill	How to Compare Population Maps	98–99
Lesson 2	Recent Immigrants to the United States	100–101
Skill	How to Understand a Time Zone Map	102–103
Lesson 3	The National Bamboo Project of Costa Rica	104
Skill	How to Read and Compare Climographs	105
Chapter Review	People and Places	106

Chapter 12

Lesson 1	Milestones in Energy	107
Skill	How to Read a Cartogram	108–109
Lesson 2	The Conflict over Tibet	110
Skill	How to Resolve Conflict	111
Lesson 3	Democracy, British vs. American Style	112
Skill	How to Form a Logical Conclusion	113
Lesson 4	Looking at the Pacific Rim	114
Chapter Review	History, Government, and Economy	115

NAME _____ DATE _____

Make Comparisons

DIRECTIONS: Look at the words below. List in Column A at least ten words that would have been most important to early human ancestors. In Column B, list at least ten words that are important to you. Then answer the questions that follow.

basketball	cave	food	homework	plants	telephone
bed	family	friends	hunting	school	television
camp	fire	home	moving	stone	water

COLUMN A		COLUMN B	
camp	hunting	basketball	homework
cave	moving	bed	school
family	plants	family	telephone
fire	stone	food	television
food	water	friends	water
friends		home	

1. What does the list in Column A tell you about the lives of early human ancestors?
Survival took up most of their time and energy. Working and living in a band was important.

2. What does the list in Column B tell you about our society today?
We have time for leisure and entertainment, but we must still meet our basic needs to survive.

3. Which words appear in both lists? Explain your answer. Students should list food and water and perhaps family and friends. Basic human physical and emotional needs do not change.

Use after reading Chapter 1, Lesson 1, pages 51–54.

How Old Is That Fossil?

Learn More About a Subject

DIRECTIONS: **Read the paragraphs. Then answer the questions.**

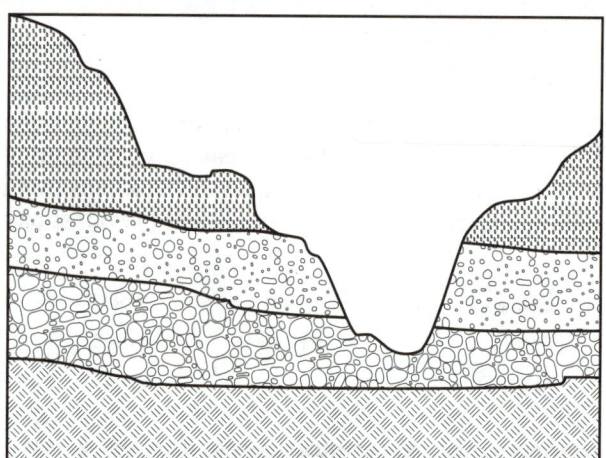

Scientists use two basic methods to figure out the age of fossils. One method is to study the layers in the Earth where the fossils are found. The other method is to measure the radioactive decay of the fossils themselves.

The older method is known as layer-dating. Earth's layers are made of different kinds of rock. Scientists know that younger rocks lie on top of older rocks. Fossils found in a lower layer are older than the fossils found in a higher layer. Fossils found in a higher layer are more recent than those found below.

Modern scientists also measure the radioactive decay in fossils to determine their age more precisely. Some chemical elements change at very predictable rates as they decay over a period of time. These rates of change vary from one element to another. For example, scientists are able to date the changes in carbon, the element found in all living plants and animals and in all fossils. Scientists can measure the rate of change in carbon for fossils 50,000 years old or younger.

Sometimes scientists combine both layer-dating and radioactive dating to measure the age of fossils older than 50,000 years. Scientists are able to measure radioactive changes in certain elements other than carbon over periods as long as hundreds of millions of years. If scientists find through radioactive dating that a rock layer is 15 million years old, they know that the fossils found below that layer are more than 15 million years old.

1. How do modern scientists determine the age of fossils?

by measuring the radioactivity of carbon; by measuring the age of Earth's layers where fossils are found

2. Why do scientists use the radioactivity of carbon to date fossils?

because carbon is present in all forms of life, and fossils are the remains of once-living things

3. What do you think fossils can tell us about life long ago?

Fossils can show what life forms lived on Earth long ago.

NAME _____ DATE _____

HOW TO USE LATITUDE AND LONGITUDE

Apply Map and Globe Skills

DIRECTIONS: On the map, study the locations of the fossil finds. Then complete the activities.

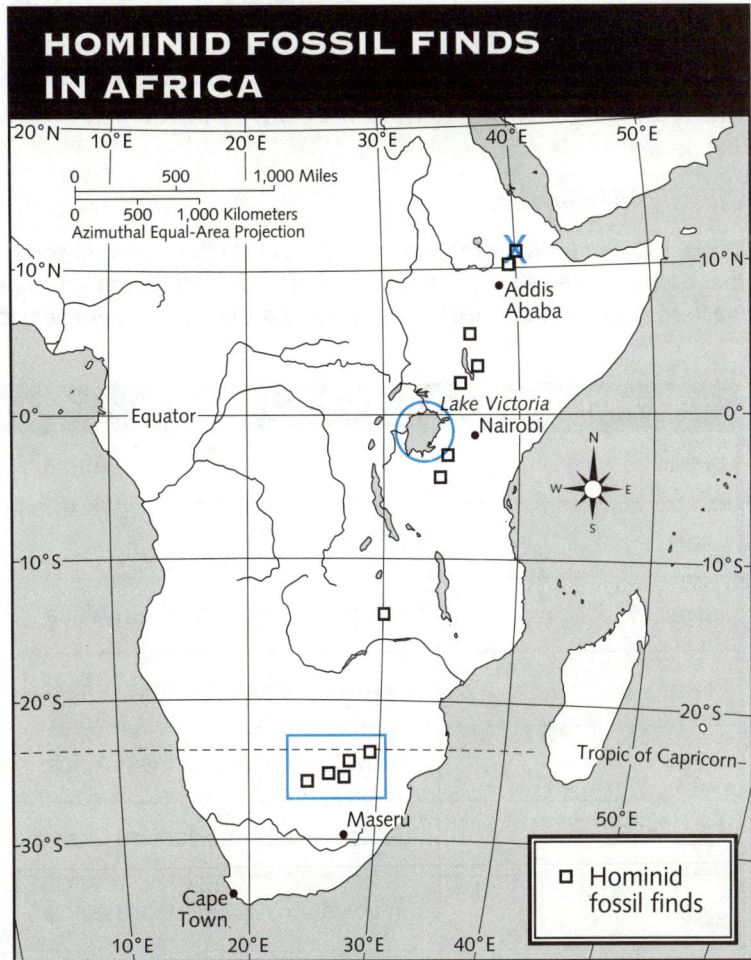

HOMINID FOSSIL FINDS IN AFRICA

1. Many hominid fossils have been found near Lake Victoria. Circle this lake on the map.

2. What special name is given to Lake Victoria's latitude? __equator__

3. Put an X through the northernmost hominid findings. Using a map of Africa, find the name of the country where these findings are located. Write the name in the space provided. __Ethiopia__

4. Draw a box around the findings that are located between 30°S and 20°S latitude.

5. Between which meridians in southern Africa were most fossils found?
   __20°E and 40°E__

Use after reading Chapter 1, Skill Lesson, pages 62–63.

NAME _____   DATE _____

Early Agriculture Around the World

All around the world early agriculture started independently. Even so, many cultures domesticated the same plants and animals.

Classify Information

DIRECTIONS: Using information from your textbook, list in the right column the area or areas that domesticated each plant and animal in the left column. The areas to choose from are southwestern Asia, northern Africa, Pakistan and China, southern Mexico, and South America.

PLANT OR ANIMAL	LOCATION
wheat	southwestern Asia, northern Africa
rice	Pakistan and China
sheep	southwestern Asia, northern Africa
barley	southwestern Asia, northern Africa
cattle	southwestern Asia, northern Africa
pigs	Pakistan and China, northern Africa
goats	southwestern Asia, northern Africa
chickens	Pakistan and China
chili peppers	southern Mexico, South America
potatoes	South America
millet	Pakistan and China
squash	southern Mexico
water buffaloes	Pakistan and China

Use after reading Chapter 1, Lesson 3, pages 64–69.

NAME _____ DATE _____

HOW TO READ A PARALLEL TIME LINE

Apply Chart and Graph Skills

DIRECTIONS: **The three-part time line on page 6 shows what was happening in different areas of life in the United States in the twentieth century. Use the time line to answer the questions below.**

1. What could kids do for fun in 1960? <u>play with toys such as the Hula Hoop™, the Slinky™, Silly Putty™, and Barbie dolls™; go to movies; watch TV</u>

2. Do you think most fans who attended the first Rose Bowl game traveled in cars? <u>No; the first Rose Bowl game was played in 1902. The Model T, the first popular car, was introduced in 1908.</u>

3. What might a sixth grader have played with at the time of the Persian Gulf War? <u>in-line skates, skateboards, or video games</u>

4. Was racial integration first achieved in sports or in schools? <u>It was first achieved in sports. Jackie Robinson played major-league baseball in 1947. Public schools were desegregated in 1954.</u>

5. Which event could Americans have watched on TV in 1969? <u>United States astronaut Neil Armstrong walking on the moon</u>

6. Do you think many people living today remember when Hawaii became a state? <u>Yes, many do. Hawaii became a state in 1959.</u>

(Continued)

Use after reading Chapter 1, Skill Lesson, pages 70–71.

NAME _____ DATE _____

UNITED STATES MAJOR EVENTS TIME LINE, 1900–PRESENT

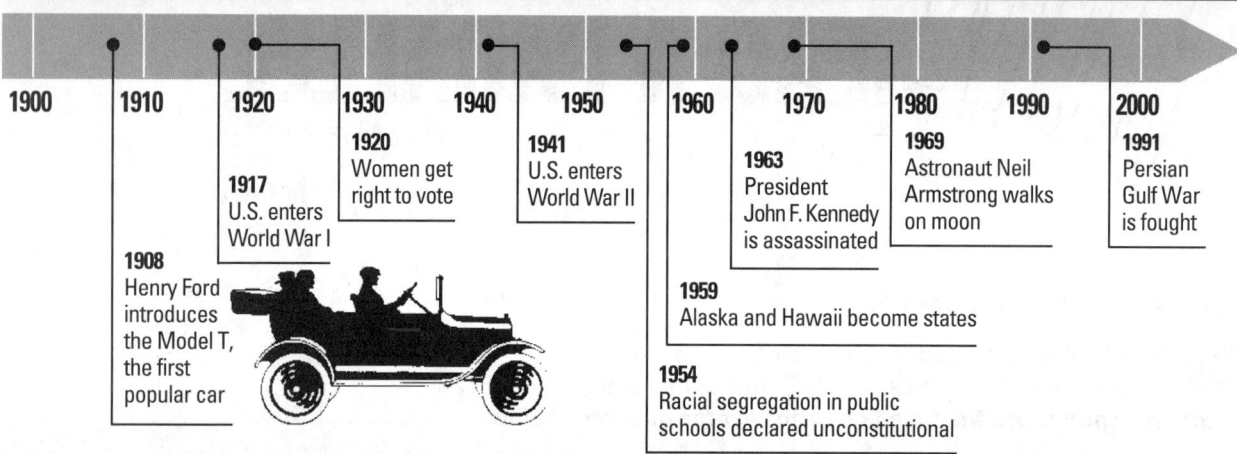

- 1908 Henry Ford introduces the Model T, the first popular car
- 1917 U.S. enters World War I
- 1920 Women get right to vote
- 1941 U.S. enters World War II
- 1954 Racial segregation in public schools declared unconstitutional
- 1959 Alaska and Hawaii become states
- 1963 President John F. Kennedy is assassinated
- 1969 Astronaut Neil Armstrong walks on moon
- 1991 Persian Gulf War is fought

UNITED STATES ENTERTAINMENT TIME LINE, 1900–PRESENT

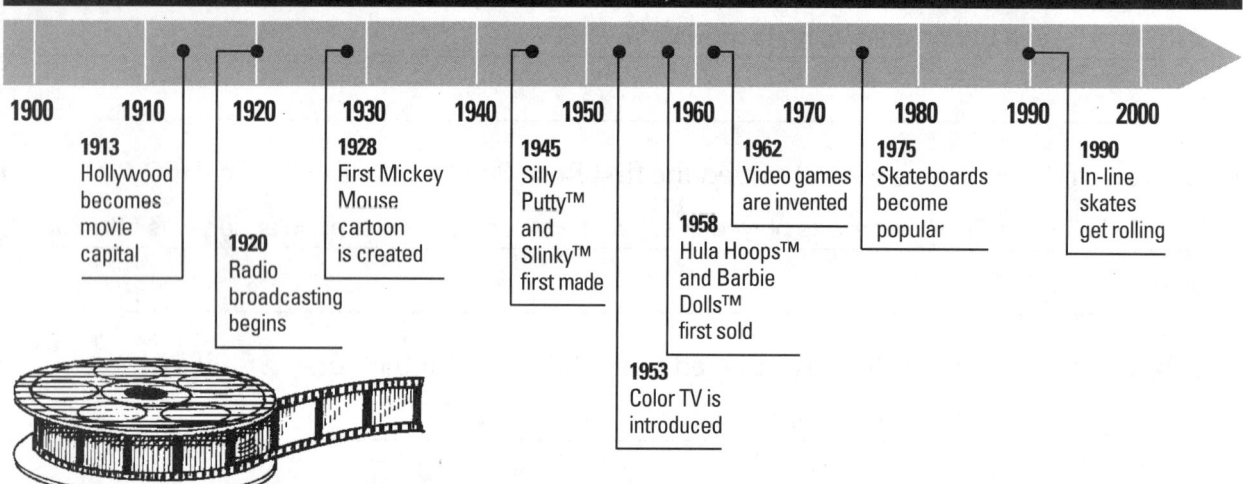

- 1913 Hollywood becomes movie capital
- 1920 Radio broadcasting begins
- 1928 First Mickey Mouse cartoon is created
- 1945 Silly Putty™ and Slinky™ first made
- 1953 Color TV is introduced
- 1958 Hula Hoops™ and Barbie Dolls™ first sold
- 1962 Video games are invented
- 1975 Skateboards become popular
- 1990 In-line skates get rolling

UNITED STATES SPORTS TIME LINE, 1900–PRESENT

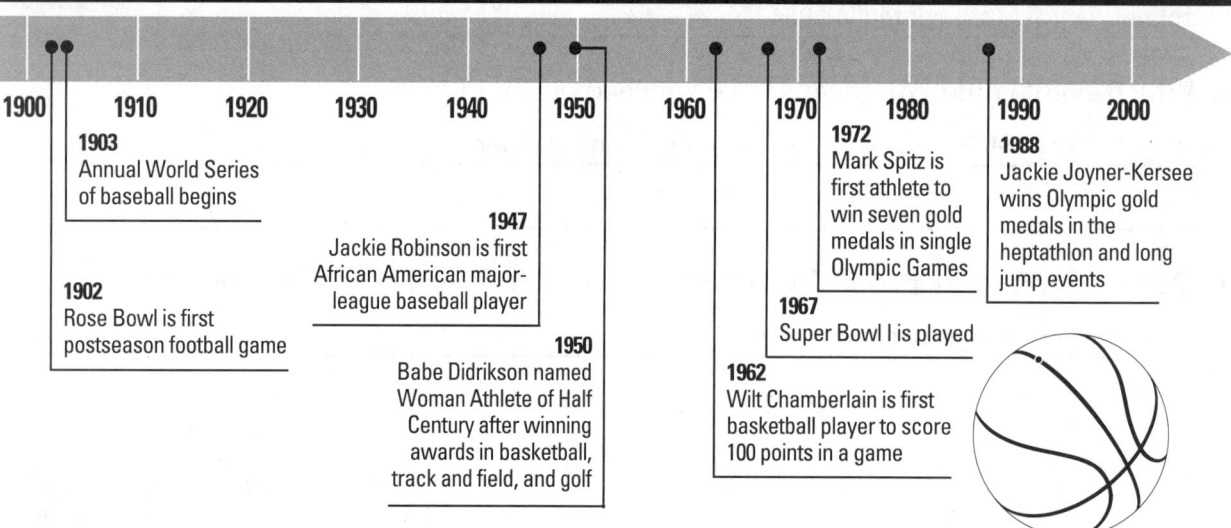

- 1902 Rose Bowl is first postseason football game
- 1903 Annual World Series of baseball begins
- 1947 Jackie Robinson is first African American major-league baseball player
- 1950 Babe Didrikson named Woman Athlete of Half Century after winning awards in basketball, track and field, and golf
- 1962 Wilt Chamberlain is first basketball player to score 100 points in a game
- 1967 Super Bowl I is played
- 1972 Mark Spitz is first athlete to win seven gold medals in single Olympic Games
- 1988 Jackie Joyner-Kersee wins Olympic gold medals in the heptathlon and long jump events

6 ACTIVITY BOOK   Use after reading Chapter 1, Skill Lesson, pages 70–71.

NAME _____ DATE _____

A PICTURE OF DAILY LIFE

When the village of Skara Brae was uncovered on an island off northern Scotland in 1850, the well-preserved ruins provided a good picture of how people had lived there.

Draw Conclusions

DIRECTIONS: Study the drawings below of things uncovered at Skara Brae. What do they tell you? Using only the evidence of the drawings, answer the questions that follow.

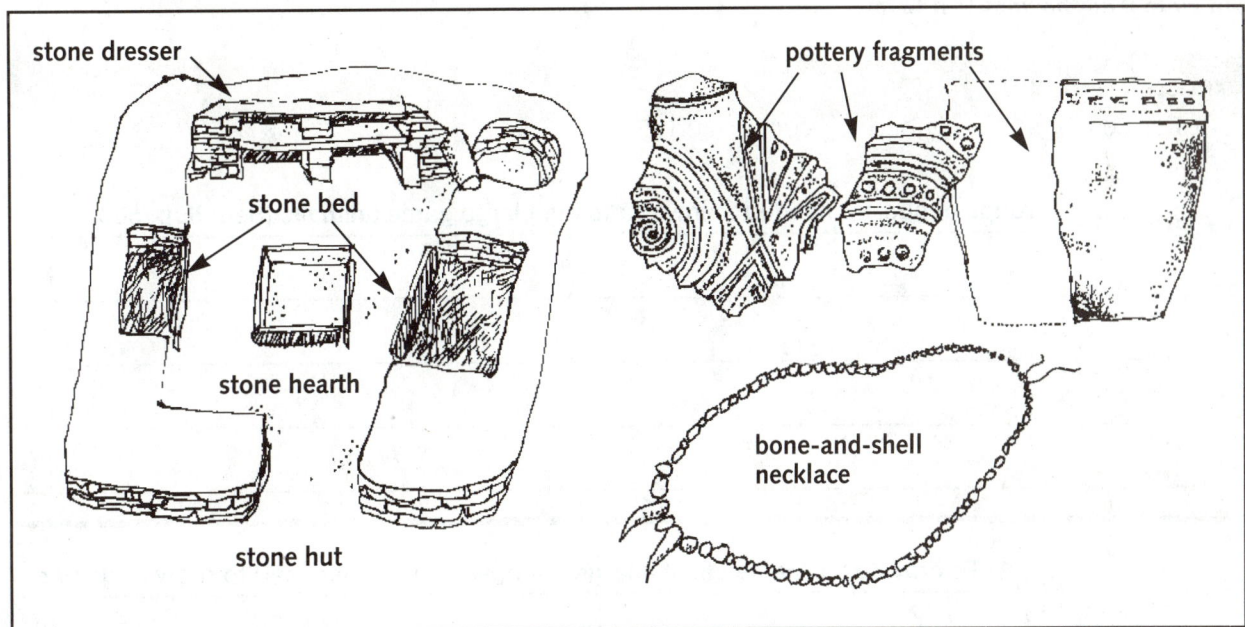

1. What material was abundant on the island? How do you know?
   stone; because the hut, beds, dresser, and hearth were all made of stone

2. What clue can you find about the cool temperature of the island's climate?
   The hearth had beds on two sides and was in the center of the hut.

3. Give two examples of evidence that the people of Skara Brae had some leisure time.
   decorated pottery and necklace

Use after reading Chapter 1, Lesson 4, pages 72–79.

NAME _____ DATE _____

HOW TO FORMULATE A Generalization

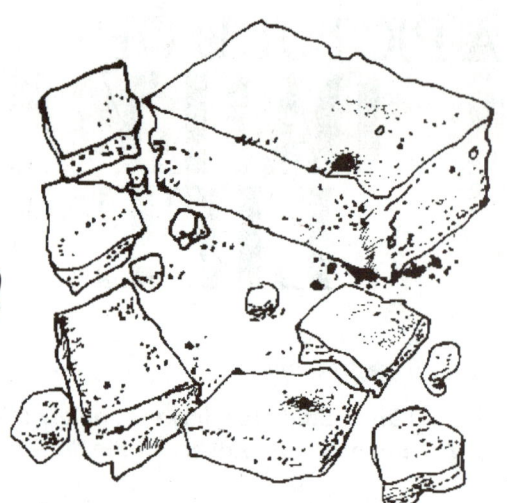

Apply Critical Thinking Skills

DIRECTIONS: Below, a generalization has been made for you. Find information in your textbook to support the generalization, and write it on the lines that follow.

Generalization:
People in early societies had to work together.

1. Hunters: Groups of hunters needed teamwork to hunt large game animals. (See PE p. 56.)

2. Early farmers: To provide for the needs of a large band, some members had to grow or gather food, while others made tools and clothing. (See PE p. 64.)

3. The village of Skara Brae: In Skara Brae everyone worked together to build houses for all. Men gathered large stones for foundations and walls. Women and children gathered smaller stones. (See PE p. 72.)

8 ACTIVITY BOOK   Use after reading Chapter 1, Skill Lesson, page 80–81.

NAME _____ DATE _____

People of the STONE AGE

Connect Main Ideas

DIRECTIONS: Use this organizer to describe the ways of life of people who lived during the Stone Age. Write two examples for each box.

First Footsteps
Modern experts have discovered much about human ancestors.

1. Students may mention archaeologists and paleoanthropologists study fossils to learn about human ancestors,
2. that these scientists have found the remains of Homo habilis and Homo erectus, their tools, and camp sites.

Early Farmers
Many early people became food producers instead of food collectors.

1. Students may mention geographic areas of earliest agriculture, reasons for development of agriculture, and effects of changing from food
2. collectors to food producers.

People of the Stone Age

Hunters and Gatherers
Early people lived and worked in groups to collect food.

1. Students may mention bands, the need to work together and the consequences of lack of cooperation, and the need to migrate as a band to
2. find food sources.

Use after reading Chapter 1, pages 50–83.

NAME _____ DATE _____

The Importance of RESOURCES

Write an Article

DIRECTIONS: Read the paragraphs. Then complete the article as directed.

Landforms, natural resources, and climate affect how people live, the work they do, and whether they live in safety or danger. The people of ancient Mesopotamia lived under very harsh conditions. They used the few natural resources the region provided, including clay, water, and soil, to help them survive in their difficult environment.

Use what you have learned to complete an article about the natural resources of ancient Mesopotamia. The article should explain how the ancient Mesopotamians used their resources and how this affected both their work and their daily lives. The article has been started for you.

CLAY, WATER, AND SOIL IN ANCIENT MESOPOTAMIA

Clay. Clay was one of the natural resources of ancient Mesopotamia. Farmers, builders, writers, travelers, and homemakers used clay in different ways. They learned to fire clay and mold it into bricks for building. They found that mixing pieces of broken brick into soil helped crops grow. They made jugs and bowls of clay to hold wheat and barley. They made clay pots that they used to cook their food. They wrote on clay tablets. The maps they drew on clay tablets helped them understand where they were and where they planned to go.

Water. Students should point out that the rivers made it possible for ancient Mesopotamians to survive. By flooding and then receding, the rivers brought silt, a natural fertilizer, to the land. Students also should point out that due to the water shortage, the people of Mesopotamia developed a technological breakthrough, a system of irrigation. Farmers were helped, and people who lived in villages became more secure because irrigation helped protect their villages from destruction by floods. Water and the control of the water permitted people to stay in one place and develop their civilization.

(Continued)

NAME _____ DATE _____

_____
_____
_____
_____
_____
_____
_____
_____
_____

Soil. *Students should indicate that the soil of Mesopotamia was enriched by the flooding waters; that it was suitable for growing crops, such as grains, vegetables, and fruits; that the soil was able to sustain grazing animals. Students should point out that having a predictable growing season and adequate food production meant that these ancient peoples were able to stay in one place, allowing their villages to grow. Students might speculate that having ample food supplies would have enriched their economy, providing goods for trade.*

_____
_____
_____
_____
_____
_____
_____
_____
_____

Use after reading Chapter 2, Lesson 1, pages 85–88.

NAME _____ DATE _____

SUMERIAN CULTURE

What did people need to build a civilization like Sumer? One thing that was very important was written language. The cuneiform writing that the Sumerians used began as pictures that stood for whole words or ideas.

Decode Cuneiform Symbols

DIRECTIONS: Imagine you are an archaeologist who has uncovered a Sumerian message from around 2400 B.C. Study the table of early cuneiform symbols. Then translate the story that follows in the space provided.

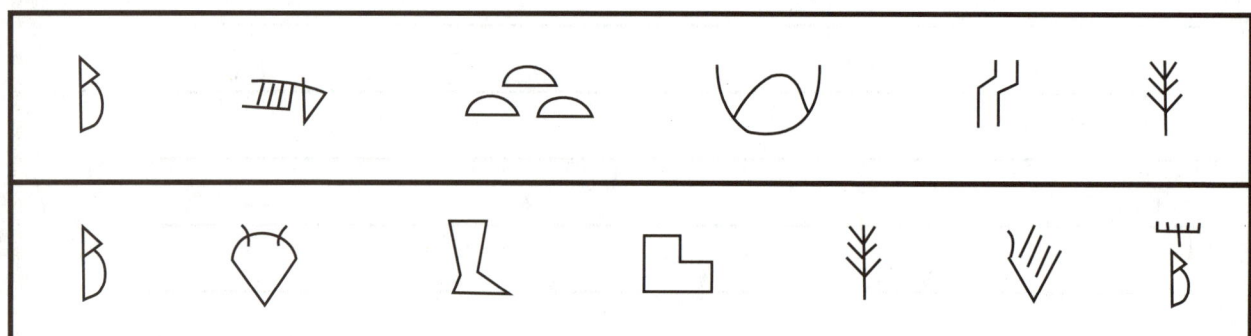

A man tilled his land. With sun and water he grew grain. The man took his ox and went to the city to give grain to the king.

12 ACTIVITY BOOK   Use after reading Chapter 2, Lesson 2, pages 89–95.

NAME _____ DATE _____

The Code of HAMMURABI

Hammurabi believed that his collection of laws would bring peace and security to the people of Babylon. By making sure that rules and punishments were the same throughout Babylon, he hoped to create an honest society and prevent the strong from taking advantage of the weak.

Use Source Material

DIRECTIONS: Some of Hammurabi's laws are given below. Read them carefully. Then follow the directions on the next page.

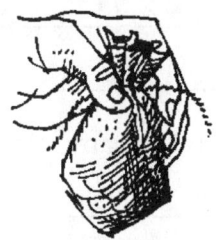

On Stealing
- 14. If a man has stolen a child, he shall be put to death.
- 22. If a man has committed highway robbery and has been caught, that man shall be put to death.

On Farming
- 42. If a man has rented a field to cultivate and has not grown any grain on the field, he shall be held responsible for not doing the work and shall pay rent.
- 48. If a man owes a debt and a storm has flooded his field or destroyed his crop, in that year he shall pay nothing.

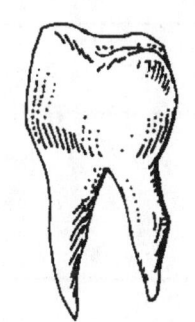

On Harming Others
- 196. If a man has knocked out the eye of a nobleman, his eye shall be knocked out.
- 198. If a man has knocked out the eye of a poor man, he shall pay one mina of silver. (A mina equals about 2 pounds.)
- 200. If a nobleman has knocked out the tooth of a man who is his equal, his tooth shall be knocked out.
- 201. If a nobleman has knocked out the tooth of a poor man, he shall pay one-third of a mina of silver.

(Continued)

NAME _____ DATE _____

DIRECTIONS: Read the statements below. Underline True **or** False *to show whether each statement agrees with what you have learned of Hammurabi's laws. Explain your answers.*

1. Stealing was not a very serious crime.

True/<u>False</u> Thieves were put to death.

2. Farmers were treated fairly.

<u>True</u>/False It seems fair not to punish a farmer if a crop was lost through a natural disaster, such as a storm. It seems fair to have to pay rent to the owner of the field if the farmer had no crop just because the farmer didn't plant it.

3. Laws against harming others were fair if they involved people within the same class.

<u>True</u>/False Law 200 shows that people in the same class were treated the same way.

4. Laws against harming others favored the poor.

True/<u>False</u> They favored the rich. People who injured members of the upper classes had to pay by suffering the same injury. People who injured the poor only had to pay money.

NAME _____ DATE _____

HOW TO COMPARE MAPS
WITH DIFFERENT PROJECTIONS

Apply Map and Globe Skills

DIRECTIONS: Study the four map projections shown below. Then in the table on the next page, place check marks in the columns that match the descriptions of the map features in the left column.

ROBINSON

VAN DER GRINTEN

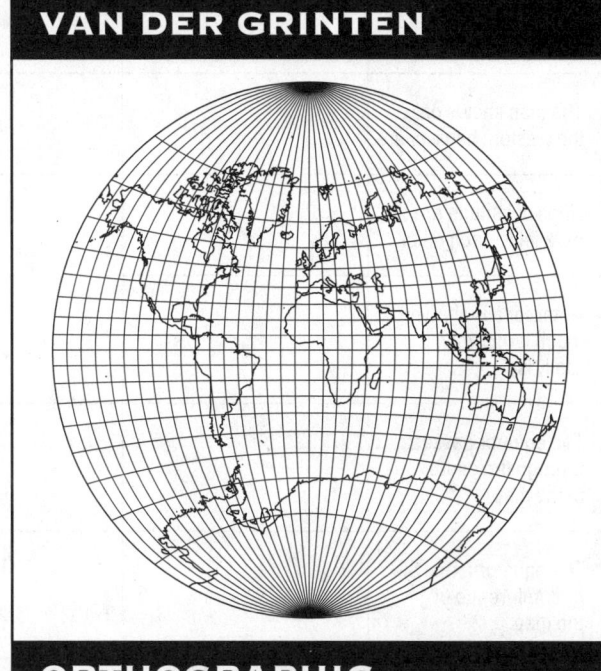

POLAR

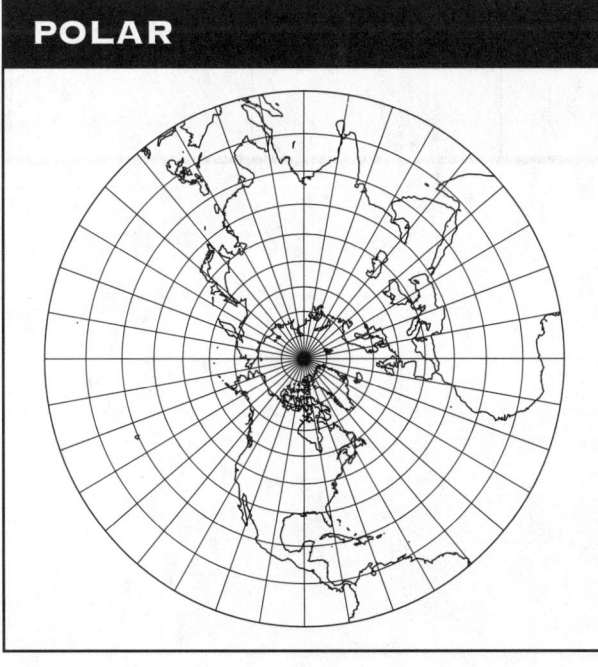

ORTHOGRAPHIC

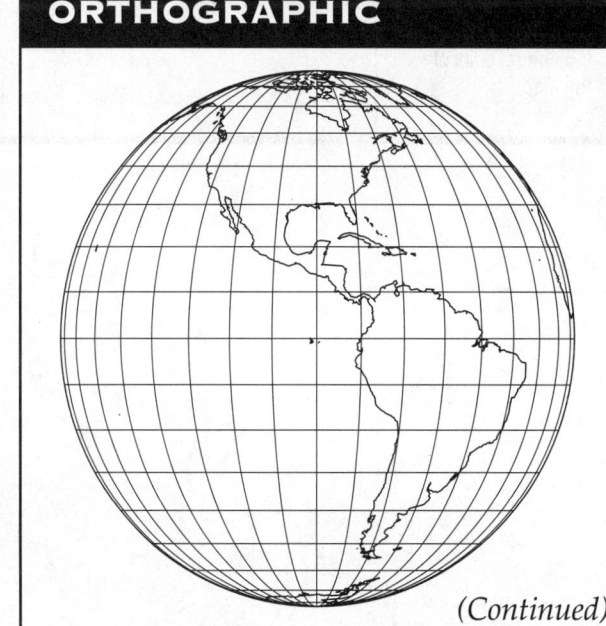

(Continued)

Use after reading Chapter 2, Skill Lesson, pages 102–104.

ACTIVITY BOOK 15

NAME _____ DATE _____

	ROBINSON	VAN DER GRINTEN	POLAR	ORTHOGRAPHIC
The map looks most like a globe.				✓
The map looks as if it were drawn looking down on the North Pole.			✓	
The North Pole is shown as a point.		✓	✓	✓
The North Pole is shown as a line.	✓			
The map shows only the western hemisphere.				✓
Lines of latitude are parallel to each other.	✓		✓	✓
Antarctica is shown much larger than it really is.	✓	✓		
The equator passes through the center of the map.	✓	✓		✓
The equator forms the circumference of the map.			✓	
The North Pole is the central point of the map.			✓	

NAME _____ DATE _____

King Solomon's TRADE AGREEMENT

About 960 B.C. King Solomon decided to build a magnificent temple. The First Book of Kings in the Bible tells how he went about it.

Use Source Material

DIRECTIONS: Read the following quotations and text. Then answer the questions on the next page.

> "Now King Hiram of Tyre sent his servants to Solomon, when he heard that they had anointed him king in place of his father; for Hiram had always been a friend to David. Solomon sent word to Hiram, saying, . . . 'I intend to build a house for the name of the Lord my God, as the Lord said to my father David. . . . Therefore command that cedars from the Lebanon be cut for me. My servants will join your servants, and I will give you whatever wages you set for your servants; for you know that there is no one among us who knows how to cut timber like the Sidonians.'" (I Kings 5:1–2, 5–6).

Hiram willingly agreed to Solomon's proposal. But as a good Tyrian trader, Hiram clearly states the benefits that both kings will receive in this friendly agreement. The First Book of Kings records Hiram's response:

> "'I have heard the message that you have sent to me; I will fulfill all your needs in the matter of cedar and cypress timber. My servants shall bring it down to the sea from the Lebanon; I will make it into rafts to go by sea to the place you indicate. I will have them broken up there for you to take away. And you shall meet my needs by providing food for my household.'" (I Kings 5:8–9).

According to the First Book of Kings, it took Solomon seven years to build the temple (I Kings 6:38). And in payment, every year Solomon gave Hiram a certain amount of food for his services, about 240,000 bushels of wheat and 240,000 gallons of pure olive oil (I Kings 5:11).

Afterward, Solomon also wanted to build a palace, so he continued to count on Hiram for the needed materials and assistance.

> "King Solomon built a fleet . . . on the shore of the Red Sea. . . . Hiram sent his servants with the fleet, sailors who were familiar with the sea, together with the servants of Solomon" (I Kings 9:26–27). "Moreover, the fleet of Hiram, which carried gold from Ophir, brought from Ophir a great quantity of almug wood and precious stones." (I Kings 10:11).

(Continued)

NAME _____ DATE _____

> "Solomon was building his own house thirteen years" (I Kings 7:1). "At the end of twenty years, in which Solomon had built the two houses, the house of the Lord and the king's house, King Hiram of Tyre having supplied Solomon with cedar and cypress timber and gold, as much as he desired, King Solomon gave to Hiram twenty cities of the land of Galilee" (I Kings 9:10–11).

1. Why was King Hiram already friendly toward King Solomon?
   Hiram had been a friend of Solomon's father, King David.

2. What was the first thing King Solomon needed for the temple?
   cedar and cypress timber

3. How did King Hiram say he would deliver the material to King Solomon?
   He would make rafts of the timber and float them on the sea to wherever Solomon wanted them.

4. What did Hiram receive in return for this service each year?
   about 240,000 bushels of wheat and about 240,000 gallons of pure olive oil

5. Why did Solomon expand his trade relationship with Hiram to the Red Sea?
   Solomon needed other materials to build a palace.

6. How long did it take to complete the temple and the palace?
   It took 7 years to complete the temple and 13 years to complete the palace, a total of 20 years.

7. How do we know that the first agreement was changed and that food from Solomon was no longer enough to cover Hiram's expenses on these projects?
   At the end of the projects, Solomon gave Hiram 20 cities in Galilee.

ACTIVITY BOOK   Use after reading Chapter 2, Lesson 4, pages 105–109.

NAME _____ DATE _____

A Time Line of Money

Sequence Events

DIRECTIONS: On the lines provided, write the missing year or years for each of the following events. Use your textbook, and clues from the information below, to fill in the missing years.

A. ___2000___ B.C. Banking exists in Babylonia with storage of valuables.

B. ___1790–1750___ B.C. Hammurabi's Code includes laws on banking.

C. ___961___ B.C. Solomon becomes King of Israel after the death of King David.

D. ___around 600___ B.C. The first coins, made of electrum, are produced in Lydia.

E. ___550___ B.C. Fifty years after introducing electrum coins, Lydians make separate gold coins and silver coins.

F. ___540___ B.C. Within ten years after their introduction, Lydian gold and silver coins are spread to distant lands by trade and warfare.

DIRECTIONS: Place the letter of each of the above events in the appropriate place on the time line below.

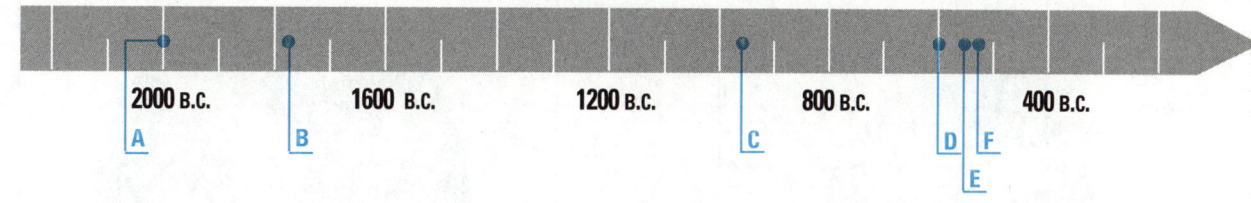

Use after reading Chapter 2, Lesson 5, pages 110–113.

NAME _____ DATE _____

HOW TO COMPARE INFORMATION WITH GRAPHS

Apply Chart and Graph Skills

DIRECTIONS: The present-day countries that occupy the ancient Fertile Crescent have differing populations. Examine the graphs below. Then answer the questions and complete the activity on the next page.

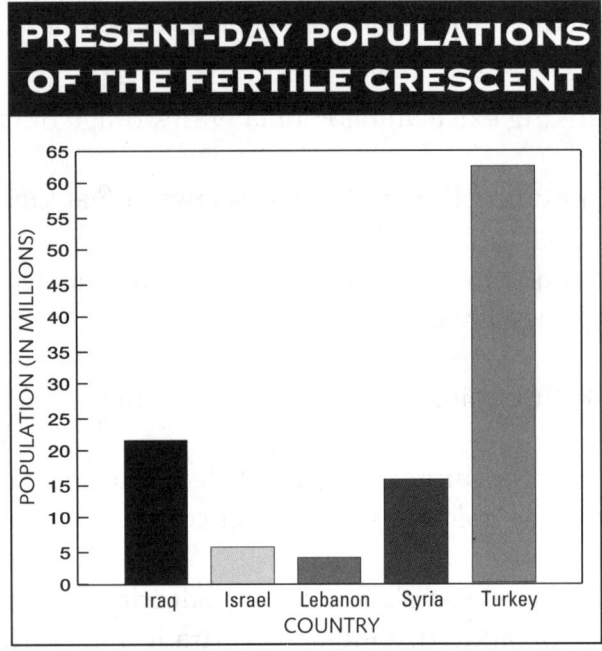

Graph A

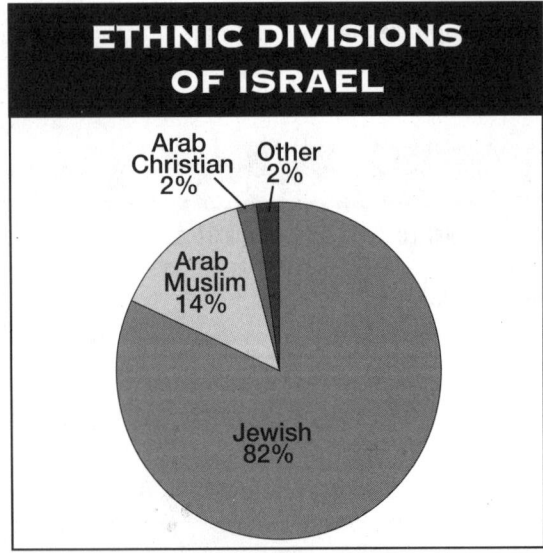

Graph B

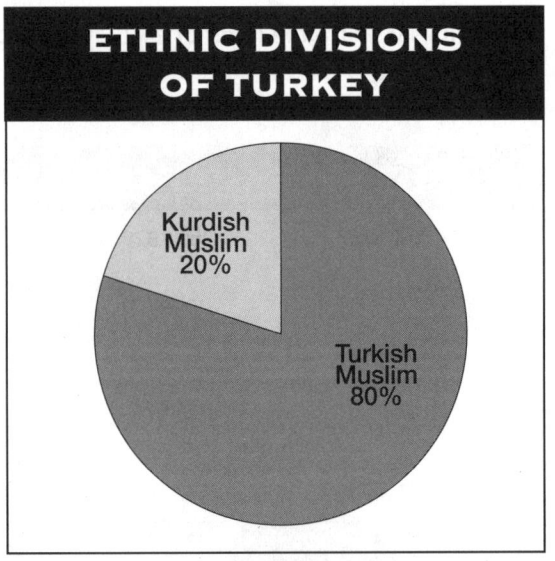

Graph C *(Continued)*

20 ACTIVITY BOOK

Use after reading Chapter 2, Skill Lesson, pages 114–115.

NAME _____ DATE _____

1. Which country has the largest population? __Turkey_____

2. Which country has the smallest population? __Lebanon_____

3. Which country has about four times as many people as the country of Israel? __Iraq__

4. Does Turkey or Israel have more ethnic diversity? __Israel_____

5. Is Turkey's Kurdish population greater or smaller in actual numbers than Israel's Jewish population? __greater_____

DIRECTIONS: Lebanon's population is 74 percent Arab Muslim, 21 percent Arab Christian, 4 percent Armenian Christian, and 1 percent other. Fill in the circle graph below to show the ethnic groups of Lebanon.

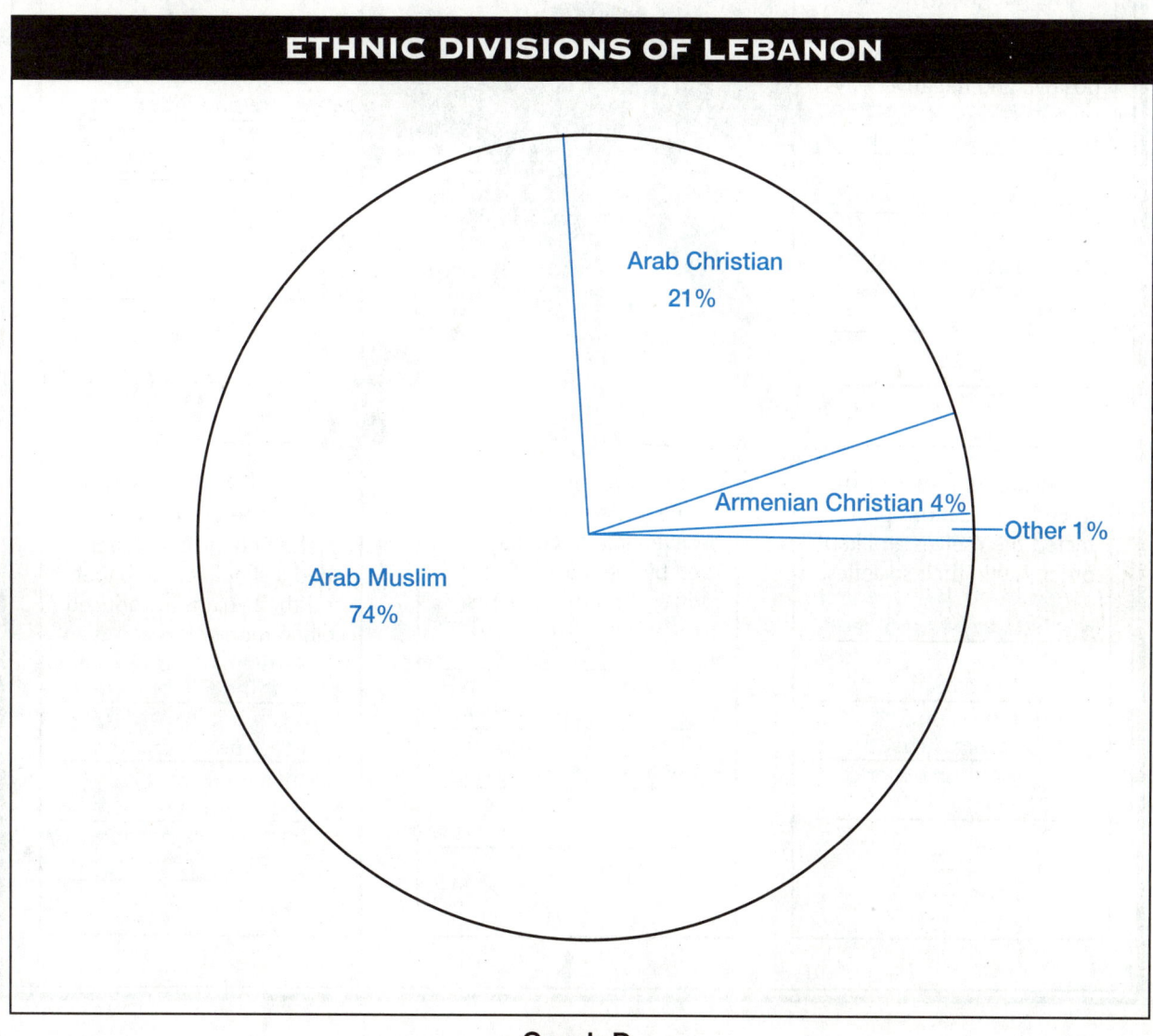

Graph D

Use after reading Chapter 2, Skill Lesson, pages 114–115.

ACTIVITY BOOK 21

NAME _____ DATE _____

SOUTHWEST ASIA

Connect Main Ideas

DIRECTIONS: Use this organizer to tell about the achievements of the early people of southwestern Asia. List two examples for each box.

Geography of Ancient Mesopotamia
The geography of the Fertile Crescent affected the people there in both positive and negative ways.
Students may mention
1. the dry soil, hot climate, and unpredictable rivers that challenged the early people of the fertile crescent to farm, build settlements, and irrigate.

Civilization in Mesopotamia
The people of ancient Sumer developed new ways of doing things.
Students may mention
1. such innovations as the wheel, the wheeled cart, flood control using dikes, ziggurats, cuneiform, and
2. government.

Conquests and Empires
Early civilizations protected themselves and kept order within their societies.
Students may mention
1. that the need for land created wars and from the wars came new weapons, empires and
2. emperors, laws, the need for order, and justice.

The Ancient Israelites
The ancient Israelites believed in one God and lived by the teachings of the Ten Commandments.
Students may mention
1. Abraham, Moses, David, and Solomon as leaders of the ancient Israelites; and the
2. division of the land of Israel into two parts.

The Phoenicians and the Lydians
The Phoenicians developed a simplified alphabet, and the Lydians introduced coined money.
Students may mention
1. that the Phoenician alphabet spread to other areas and that the coined money of
2. the Lydians helped traders to set prices for goods and services.

22 ACTIVITY BOOK

Use after reading Chapter 2, pages 84–117.

NAME _____ DATE _____

EGYPT AND THE NILE

Map Skill *Locate Places on a Map*

DIRECTIONS: The Nile River was the heart of ancient Egyptian civilization. It ran through the center of Egypt's land and greatly influenced the Egyptian way of life. Using information from your textbook, complete the following activities.

1. Trace the path of the Nile River with a blue pencil or marker.

2. To where does the Nile River flow? __the Mediterranean Sea__ Label it on the map.

3. Draw a triangle around the Nile Delta and label it.

4. Label the area called Lower Egypt on the map.

5. Label the area called Upper Egypt on the map.

6. Why was the Nile River important to ancient Egypt? The river carried silt, a natural fertilizer. Each year the river would flood the land. Then when the flooding subsided, the silt left behind made the soil excellent for growing crops.

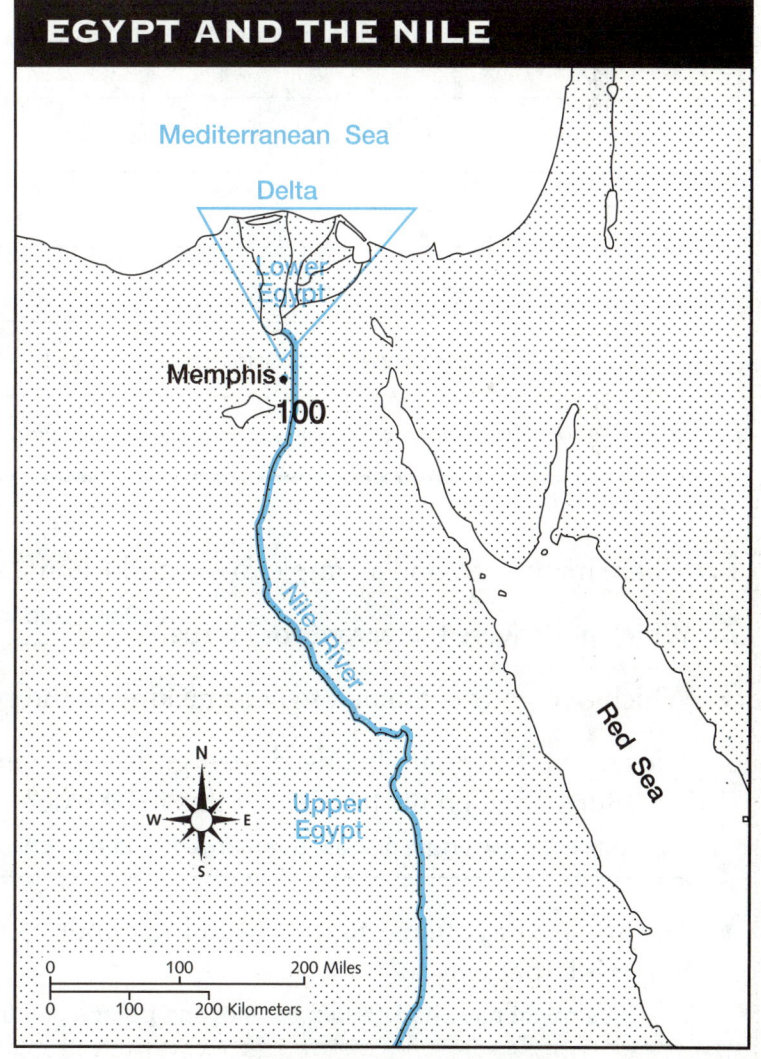

Use after reading Chapter 3, Lesson 1, pages 131–134.

NAME _____ DATE _____

THE GODS OF ANCIENT EGYPT

Interpret a Table

DIRECTIONS: Study the table about the gods of ancient Egypt. Then answer the questions that follow.

\	GODS OF ANCIENT EGYPT	
NAME	**DESCRIPTION**	**PLACE OF THE GOD**
Amon	God of wind, who later joined with Re to become Amon-Re, the king of the gods	Thebes
Hathor	Goddess of love, dance, and women, often shown in the form of a cow	Thebes
Horus	Sky god, whose eyes were thought to be the sun and the moon, sometimes shown as a falcon	Giza
Isis	Goddess of weaving, mother of Horus, wife of Osiris	Philae
Khons	Moon god, son of Amon	Karnak
Osiris	God of the dead, father of Horus	Abydos and Philae
Re	Sun god, later joined with Amon, sometimes shown as a falcon	Heliopolis
Thoth	God of wisdom and holy writings, sometimes shown in the form of a baboon	Hermopolis

1. Where might you find a temple to the god Khons? **Karnak**

2. Which gods were the parents of Horus? **Osiris and Isis**

3. Which two gods combined to become king of the gods? **Amon, Re**

4. The ancient Egyptians believed their gods lived very much like humans. How does the information on the table show this to be true?
   The gods lived in certain places, got married, and had children.

5. The ancient Egyptians often showed their gods as real and imagined animals. Why do you think that was so?
   The gods might have had certain powers and personality traits connected with the animals.

NAME _____ DATE _____

More About PYRAMIDS

Compare and Contrast

DIRECTIONS: Egyptian pyramids differed from Mesopotamian ziggurats in many ways. Use your textbook and any other resources to learn whether each statement below applies to a pyramid or to a ziggurat. Then, write a P for pyramid or Z for ziggurat on the line.

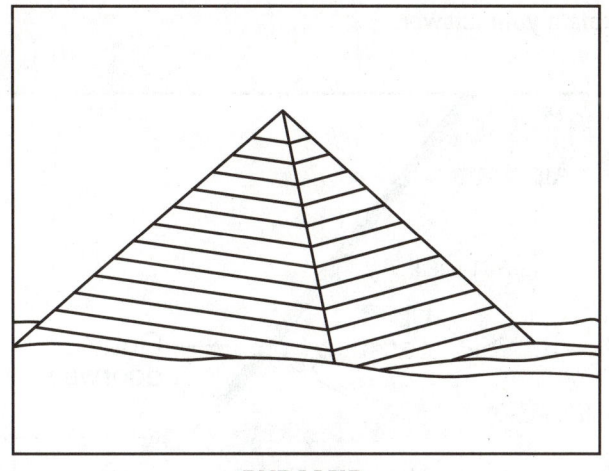

PYRAMID   **ZIGGURAT**

1. __P__ Tomb for the dead
2. __Z__ Center of activity in the city
3. __Z__ Temple to a god with an altar on top
4. __P__ Clothing, jewelry, furniture, and games were placed inside
5. __P__ Outer sides too smooth to climb
6. __P__ Built tall to reach toward heaven
7. __P__ Prayers from the *Book of the Dead* sometimes carved on its walls
8. __Z__ Workshops and temples built around its base

(Continued)

Use after reading Chapter 3, Lesson 3, pages 141–147.

NAME _____ DATE _____

The Great Pyramid at Giza, the burial place of Khufu, was completely sealed for thousands of years. Its entrance was hidden behind a layer of smooth limestone. Around 820, invaders blasted their way into the pyramid, hoping to find treasure. Today, many scholars are uncertain why the Great Pyramid of Giza was designed as it was. For example, they question the presence of air shafts and a well shaft. Some argue that the pyramid's use was for more than a tomb. Others argue that the pyramid was never meant to be entered.

Interpret a Diagram

DIRECTIONS: *Study the diagram of the Great Pyramid. Then, on the lines below, write whether you think the pyramid was used for more than a tomb. Explain your answer.*

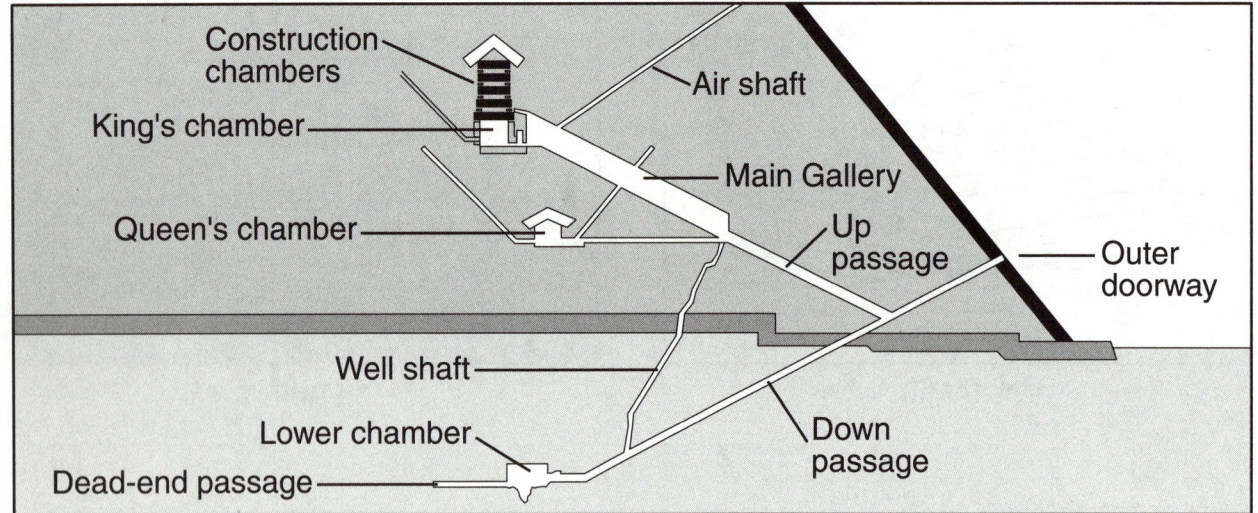

Students' answers will vary but should include something about the design of the pyramid.

26 ACTIVITY BOOK   Use after reading Chapter 3, Lesson 3, pages 141–147.

NAME _____ DATE _____

HOW TO SOLVE A PROBLEM

Apply Critical Thinking Skills

DIRECTIONS: Look at the inventor's thought list below and the five steps in problem solving. Put the inventor's thoughts in order by writing the letter of each one next to the correct step in the problem-solving process.

Invented by the ancient Egyptians, a shaduf is a tool for getting water. The shaduf helped solve one major problem for early Egyptian farmers. They needed to get water from irrigation canals that were lower than the fields.

Shaduf Inventor's Thought List

a. I could pull up buckets of water with a rope. Perhaps I could tie a bucket to a pole and lift the bucket out of the water. Or I could use the pole as a lever to lift the bucket out of the canal.

b. I gathered buckets, rope, and wooden poles. I took a sturdy pole with a bucket tied to one end and a stone weight on the other. I built a crossbar to support the pole. Now I can lift the bucket and swing it over to water my field.

c. I built my invention and tried it. It works perfectly.

d. It is easier to use a lever with a bucket tied to the end than to drag buckets up with a rope. To make the lifting even easier, I could use a heavy rock to weight the other end of the pole.

e. How do I get water into my field during a drought? The water in the irrigation canal is lower than my field.

FIVE-STEP PROBLEM SOLVING

__e__ 1. Identify the problem.

__a__ 2. Think of possible solutions.

__d__ 3. Compare the solutions, and choose the best one.

__b__ 4. Plan a way to carry out the solution.

__c__ 5. Try your solution, and think about how well it solves the problem.

In Memory of King Tutankhamen

Understand a Historical Figure

DIRECTIONS: Read the following fictional autobiography of King Tutankhamen. Then answer the questions on the following page.

As I look back now from the realm of the gods, I believe my most difficult time as pharaoh came when I was 12 years old. I'd been king for only three years when I had to make an important decision. Should I open the shrines of Osiris and the other gods that King Akhenaton had closed? Or should I follow Akhenaton's example and insist that the people forget the ancient gods and worship only the god Aton?

My vizier, Ay, told me that the priests, the army, and many other people thought that Akhenaton was a heretic who had no right to close the shrines. Ay also warned that I would bring harm to the country if I turned my back on our ancient gods. Clearly, if I did not open the shrines, I would make all of Egypt my enemy.

On the other hand, I was part of Akhenaton's family. His daughter was to be my wife. If I opened the shrines that he closed, I would make powerful enemies within the family. The priests of Aton and the court officials who had served Akhenaton would hate me.

For the good of Egypt, I knew I had to open the shrines once again. In those days, I thought that I was young and could put off giving the order to begin building my tomb. Now I see how an unpopular decision can shorten a pharaoh's reign.

But I was a god, and gods don't fear death. Yet, even gods want their deeds remembered. I am convinced that those who erase the names of past pharaohs from history are the ones who really harm Egypt. They had already begun on Akhenaton. And I was right to suspect that they would do the same to me. When Horemheb became pharaoh, he went about destroying every monument ever built in my honor. That is why I was quite happy when the stonecutters working near my tomb accidentally covered the entrance. The tomb remained sealed for 33 centuries until it was discovered in 1922 by Howard Carter.

(Continued)

NAME _____ DATE _____

    Of course, Carter's team was thrilled to find the golden death mask and thousands of carved and golden objects. But what really delighted me was their discovery of the wine jars. They had date labels that told them I had ruled for nine years until my death in 1322 B.C. Finally, history would remember me for trying to do the right thing. I was also pleased when they found my fan. An inscription on its handle told them how much I enjoyed hunting in Heliopolis. Even gods have a human side. That was obvious, too, when they found that I was once a child who had fun with a toy box, a paint set, and games.

1. How long did King Tutankhamen reign, and when did he die?
He reigned for nine years and died in 1322 B.C.

2. What was the hardest decision of King Tutankhamen's life? He had to decide between opening the shrines of Osiris and the other gods or leaving them closed as Akhenaton had done.

3. Why was this decision so difficult? He would make enemies no matter what he decided.

4. How old was King Tutankhamen when he faced that decision? He was 12 years old.

5. Using information in this autobiography, figure out how old King Tutankhamen was when he died. He was 18 years old.

6. Why was King Tutankhamen's tomb undiscovered for 33 centuries?
The tomb's entrance had been accidentally covered by stonecutters.

7. Who discovered King Tutankhamen's tomb, and in what year? Howard Carter discovered the tomb in 1922.

8. What artifacts helped date King Tutankhamen's reign? the wine jars

9. What artifacts give us some personal information about King Tutankhamen?
the fan with the inscription on its handle about hunting, and the toy box, paint set, and games

Use after reading Chapter 3, Lesson 4, pages 150–155.

NAME _____   DATE _____

THE PHARAOH QUEEN

At her coronation Hatshepsut wore more than fancy clothes and jewelry. The things she wore symbolized what the pharaoh's authority meant to Egypt. No one who saw the new pharaoh doubted that she would rule with the power of the gods of Egypt.

Classify Information

DIRECTIONS: Read the list of things that a pharaoh symbolized to the people of Egypt. Look at the drawing of Hatshepsut. Decide what each item she is wearing symbolizes. Write the symbol's number on the blank line next to each item's description.

Symbols of Pharaoh's Authority and Power

1. Symbol of Osiris's immortality represented by the pharaoh

2. Symbol of political unity between Upper and Lower Egypt

3. Symbol of the gods' protection of the pharaoh

4. Symbol of Egypt's wealth and power

5. Symbol of the pharaoh's masculine strength

Queen Hatshepsut and Her Adornments

__2__ Double crown, representing Upper Egypt and Lower Egypt

__3__ Sacred cobra, on the front of the crown, that spits poisonous fire at anyone coming too near the pharaoh

__5__ Royal braided beard

__1__ Two scepters, emblems of Osiris: the golden crook and the golden flail

__4__ Gold-and-jeweled pendant

__4__ Gold bracelets and rings

__5__ Short kilt of a king

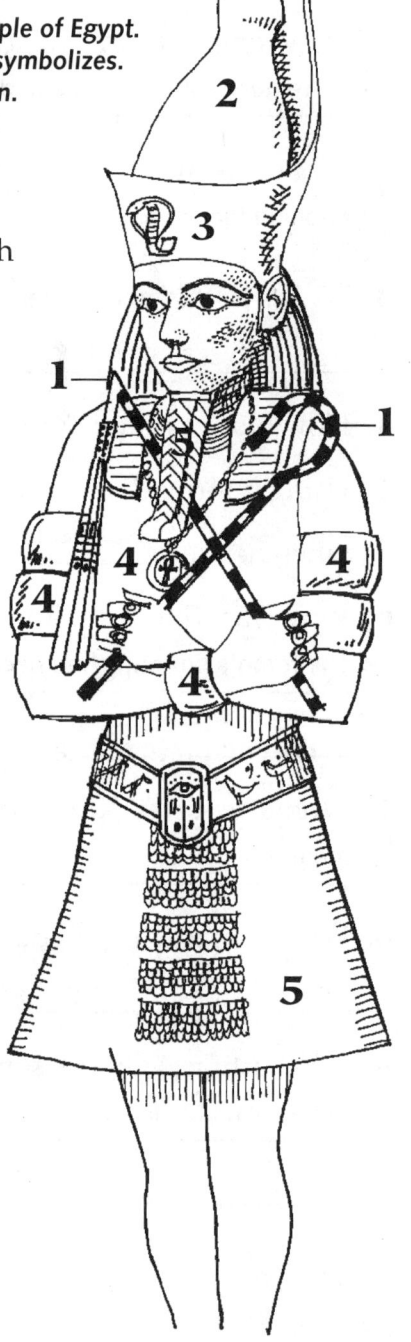

30 ACTIVITY BOOK   Use after reading Chapter 3, Lesson 5, pages 156–161.

NAME _____ DATE _____

HOW TO FOLLOW ROUTES ON A MAP

You are an Egyptian trader in 1000 B.C., carrying a load of spices, ebony, and ostrich feathers. You are on your way to meet a Phoenician ship at a seaport on the Mediterranean Sea.

Apply Map and Globe Skills

DIRECTIONS: Use the compass rose on the map to the right to chart your course. As you read the description of the trip below, fill in the names of the places you visit on the lines to the right.

You start from Thebes. You travel northwest for about 150 miles. You reach (1), where you buy food and supplies.

You then travel east for 160 miles, and you arrive at (2). Here you meet a longtime friend who has come from the Sinai Desert. He has turquoise and copper to trade. You exchange some ebony for turquoise.

At dawn you travel northwest for a distance of about 225 miles. When you finally reach (3), you are extremely tired. At dawn, after a much-needed rest, you set off 90 miles northeast to (4) to visit your sick uncle.

You prepare to leave before sunrise. Then you head northwest for about 120 miles. You finally reach the end point of your trip—the seaport (5). There your goods are put on a trading ship that will go to faraway ports.

1. Akhetaton
2. Myos Hormos
3. Memphis
4. Tanis
5. Alexandria

Use after reading Chapter 3, Skill Lesson, pages 162–163.

ACTIVITY BOOK 31

ANCIENT EGYPT

Connect Main Ideas

DIRECTIONS: Use this organizer to describe the ancient Egyptian civilization that arose in northern Africa. Write two details to support each main idea.

Geography of Northern Africa
The changing environment of the Sahara and the Nile Valley helped Egypt prosper.

1. Students may mention the migration of the early people to the Nile Valley when the Sahara dried up and that the annual flooding of the
2. Nile River brought rich silt that fertilized the land.

Importance of the Nile River
The Nile River affected the development of Egyptian society and religion.

1. Students may mention that the Nile was the "giver of life" for the ancient Egyptians, that it served as a highway to bring the Egyptian people together, and that
2. the Egyptians divided their year into three seasons based on the actions of the Nile River.

Ancient Egypt

Early Egyptian Rule
Egyptian pharaohs used different methods to build political power and religious authority.

1. Students may mention that the Egyptians believed their pharaoh was a god in human form; that the pharaohs looked for natural resources outside of
2. Egypt, and that the step pyramids were built to help the pharaoh reach Amon-Re.

Later Egyptian Rule
The Egyptians kept their civilization as it was for thousands of years yet also changed some things to meet new conditions.

1. Students may mention that at the end of the Old Kingdom, ancient Egypt was torn by civil war; that trade expanded during the Middle Kingdom; that
2. the New Kingdom saw a woman pharaoh and the introduction of monotheism.

NAME _____ DATE _____

The People of Nubia

Create an Outline

DIRECTIONS: One way to summarize information is to prepare an outline. You may recall that in an outline, you can use Roman numerals (I, II, III), capital letters (A, B, C), Arabic numerals (1, 2, 3), and lowercase letters (a, b, c). Below is an outline of this lesson that has been partly filled in. Use your textbook to complete this outline by filling in the missing titles of the subsections and other facts. On a separate sheet of paper, create an outline for the second lesson of the chapter. Use the Lesson 1 outline as a guide.

I. Chapter 4: Ancient Nubia

A. Lesson 1: Nubia: Egypt's Rival

   1. The Land and People of Ancient Nubia

      a. Ancient Nubians make pottery as early as 6000 B.C.

      b. By 2600 B.C., _Egyptians claim the trade routes in northern Nubia and help themselves to Nubia's natural resources._

   2. Freedom and Reconquest

      a. The new kingdom of Kush arises in Upper Nubia.

      b. _Kush, or the Kerma culture, prospers and supports the Hyksos, enemies of the Egyptians._

      c. The Egyptians, successful in battle, retake Nubia and rule it for about 550 years.

   3. Conquest of Egypt

      a. Kush kings rule Egypt and become Egypt's Dynasty 25.

      b. _Kings of Dynasty 25 restore Egypt to its former glory._

   4. _Kushite Rule Ends in Egypt_

      a. _Assyrians invade Egypt and defeat the combined Kushite and Egyptian armies._

      b. _Kushites learn iron making from the Assyrians._

Use after reading Chapter 4, Lesson 1, pages 167–173.

NAME _____ DATE _____

More About Kush

Link Cause and Effect

DIRECTIONS: A place's geography, history, and economy often affect one another. This was true for Kush. Fill in the missing information to show how Kush's history, geography, and economics were connected.

1. Historic event: In 671 B.C. the Assyrians defeated the Kushites.

   Economic effect: The Kushites learned to make **iron.**

2. Geographic fact: Kush was located along the Nile River, between Egypt to the north and many other peoples to the south and west.

   Economic effect: **Kush's location allowed the exchange of goods from different parts of Africa.**

3. Geographic fact: **Kush had large iron ore deposits.**

   Economic effect: Many people worked as iron ore miners and iron crafters.

4. Historic event: **Kush moved its capital to Meroë.**

   Economic effect: Meroë became a great industrial and trading center.

5. Economic fact: Merchants needed to record their business transactions.

   Historic effect: **The people of Meroë created the first Nubian written language.**

6. Historic event: Greek rulers decided to build ports on the Red Sea.

   Economic effect: **Traders turned from land to sea routes, and Meroë was no longer on a trade route.**

(Continued)

34 ACTIVITY BOOK

Use after reading Chapter 4, Lesson 2, pages 176–179.

NAME _____ DATE _____

7. Historic event: Axum defeated Kush.

Economic effect: The Kushite economy, along with its culture, was destroyed.

DIRECTIONS: *Until recently, few people knew anything about Kush. What were the causes for this? Write a paragraph with reasons why you think it has taken a long time for scholars to learn about Kush.*

Paragraphs might include the facts that the Kush language is not yet fully understood, that the Kush culture was destroyed by the people of Axum, and that the sites of the Kush cities are hard to reach. Other reasons that students may learn from research are that the modern government of Sudan may not be cooperative and that scholars may have been more interested in studying the ancient Egyptians than in studying the other ancient peoples of Africa.

Use after reading Chapter 4, Lesson 2, pages 176–179.

NAME _____   DATE _____

HOW TO USE A HISTORICAL MAP

Apply Map and Globe Skills

DIRECTIONS: Many changes have occurred on the continent of Africa since the 1950s. In 1950 nearly all the countries of Africa were colonies of European powers. One by one, the African nations have gained their independence. Study the map to the right and answer the questions that follow.

1. In 1950 how many countries of Africa were independent? __4__

2. Name the independent countries. __Egypt, Ethiopia (Eritrea was a part of Ethiopia in 1950), South Africa, and Liberia__

3. Name the two European powers that controlled most of Africa. __France and Britain__

4. What did Nigeria and Kenya have in common? __Both were colonies of Britain.__

5. The Democratic Republic of the Congo was a colony of which European country? __Belgium__

NAME _____ DATE _____

Ancient Nubia

Connect Main Ideas

DIRECTIONS: Use this organizer to tell about the ancient people of Kush and about their achievements. Write three details to support each main idea.

Ancient Nubia

Nubia: Egypt's Rival
The people of Nubia and the people of Egypt affected each other.
1. Possible answers: Empire-building pharaohs invaded Nubia; Kush's armies took over Egypt; merchants
2. exchanged goods; Nubia borrowed Egyptian clothes, writing, religion
3. _____

Kush and the World
The location and natural resources of Meroë affected the rise and fall of the Kushite culture.
1. Possible answers: Meroë had an ideal location for overland trade and became a major trading city;
2. items made from iron came from Meroë; with new water ports for trade, Meroë was no longer center of
3. trade and Kush culture fell

Use after reading Chapter 4, pages 166–183.

ACTIVITY BOOK 37

Harcourt Brace School Publishers

NAME _____ DATE _____

RIVERS of INDIA

Gather Information from a Map

DIRECTIONS: Rivers have been extremely important to the Indian subcontinent throughout history. Use the map on the next page to complete this activity. You may want to refer to your textbook and to an atlas or a globe as you work.

1. On the map on the next page, write the names of the present-day countries that make up the Indian subcontinent. (India, Pakistan, Bangladesh)

2. Label the two major rivers of the subcontinent. Then trace them in blue. What are their names? Indus River and Ganges River

3. Which river would an ancient trader have followed from the Himalayas to the Arabian Sea? Indus River

4. Mount Everest, the highest place on Earth, is in the Himalayas on the border of Nepal and China. Show and label Mount Everest on the map. Look up the approximate latitude and longitude of Mount Everest, and write it here. about 28°N, 87°E

5. How do the Himalayas affect the rivers of India?
Rainfall from the Himalayas flows into the rivers, causing them to rise and flood.
The Indus and Ganges rivers begin in the Himalayas.

6. How did the flooding rivers help the farmers of ancient India?
Flooding rivers brought silt, which fertilized lands in the river valleys and helped crops of cotton, sesame, wheat, and barley grow.

7. Why did large empires form in northern India rather than farther south?
Northern lands were flat and open, making farming easy. Southern lands were very uneven, making travel and farming difficult.

8. Why was the Indian subcontinent named for a river?
The people of India believed that the rivers made life possible and thought of the rivers as holy.
Rivers were very important for the survival of the ancient people, for their farming and travel.

(Continued)

NAME _____   DATE _____

9. What dangers have rivers and monsoons presented to the people of India?
   Floods have destroyed homes, sometimes entire villages, and changed the course of the rivers.

10. What is deforestation, and how does it affect the patterns of river flow?
    Deforestation is the widespread cutting down of trees. This has led to larger and larger
    flooding. Without trees in place, the flooding washes away the top layer of soil.

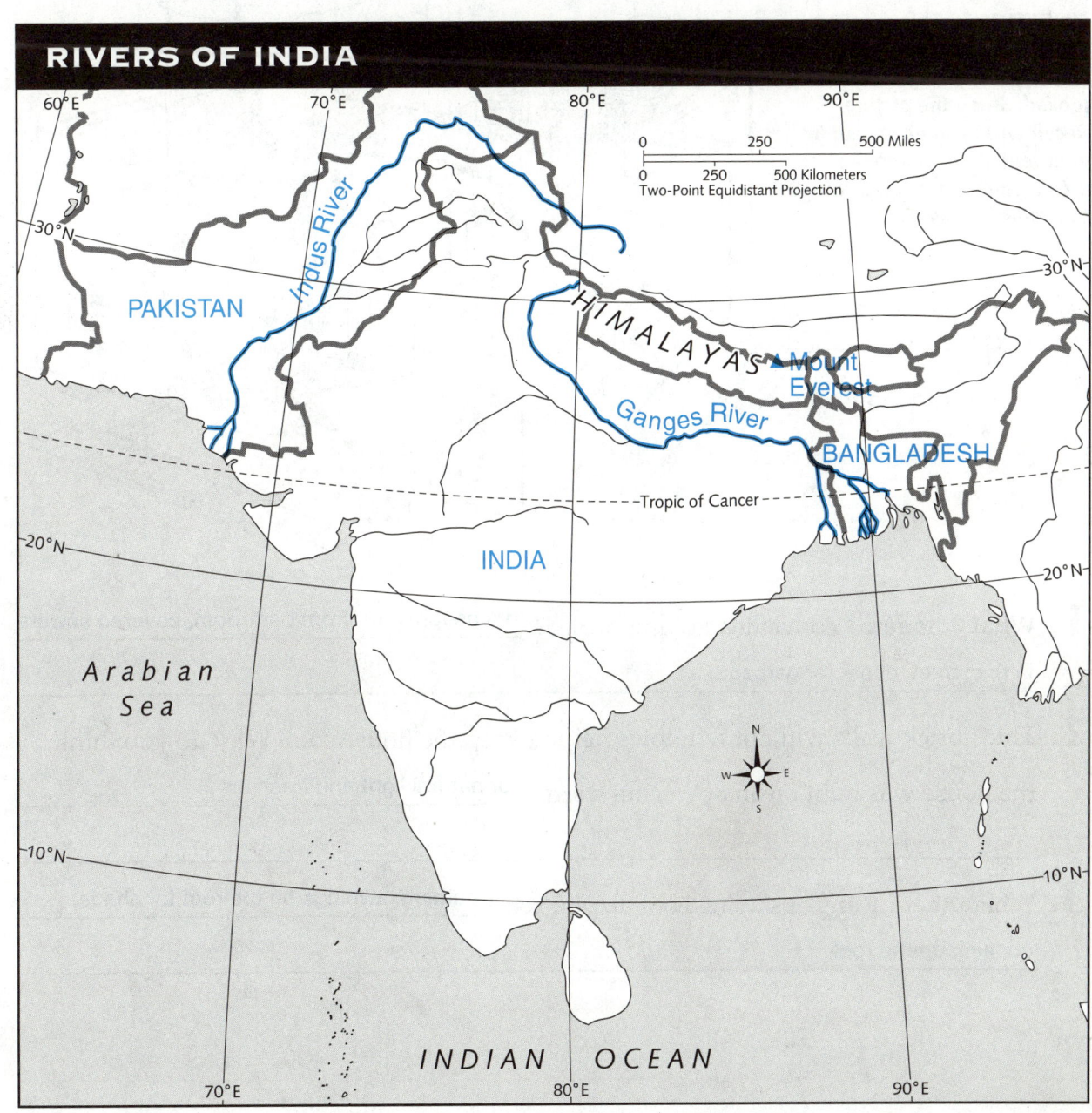

Use after reading Chapter 5, Lesson 1, pages 199–203.

NAME _____ DATE _____

Life in the City

Archaeologists first excavated the Harappan cities of the Indus Valley in the 1920s and 1930s. Walled cities, about 3 miles (5 km) in diameter, contained government buildings, a huge grain shed on a raised upper level, and wide streets laid out in squares. Life in Harappan cities was well advanced for its time.

Make Observations

DIRECTIONS: This drawing shows how a house in a Harappan city may have looked. Study the picture. Recall what you have read in your text about Harappan architecture. Then answer the questions below.

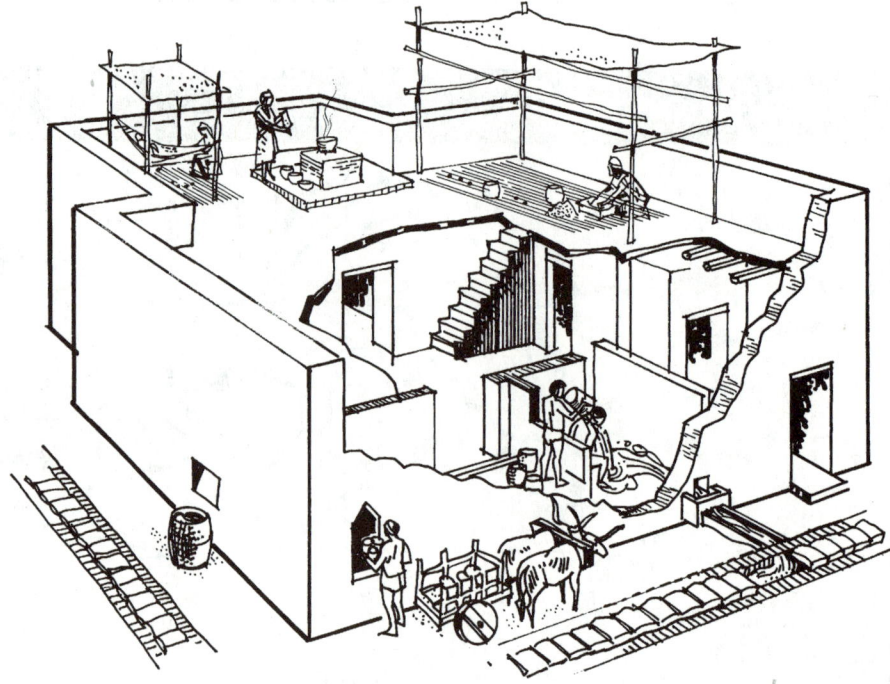

1. What "modern" conveniences do you see? drains for water from bathroom, covered sewers in the street, chute for garbage

2. Thick brick walls without windows helped keep the house cool. Why do you think the house was built on an open courtyard? for natural light and fresh air

3. What other means of staying cool do you see? bathing, awnings on the roof for shade, cooking on the roof

A Family of Languages

Almost half the people in the world today speak an Indo-European language. English is an Indo-European language. So is Hindi, which is spoken by many people in India. Hindi is one of the modern languages that came from Sanskrit, the ancient language that one group of Indo-Europeans, the Aryans, brought to India.

Find Similarities

DIRECTIONS: *The table below has a column for each of five languages. The first four columns show some common words in Sanskrit, Greek, Latin, and German. These four languages, as well as English, are from the Indo-European family of languages. See how the words are alike. In each space in the English column, write the English word that you think fits. The words in the box below may help you.*

brother	mother	sister
daughter	new	three
father	seven	

SANSKRIT	GREEK	LATIN	GERMAN	ENGLISH
matar	meter	mater	mutter	mother
pitar	pater	pater	vater	father
bhratar	adelphos	frater	bruder	brother
svasar	adelphe	soror	schwester	sister
duhitar	thugater	filia	tochter	daughter
navos	neos	novus	neu	new
trayas	treis	tres	drei	three
sapta	hepta	septem	sieben	seven

Use after reading Chapter 5, Lesson 3, pages 210–215.

NAME _____ DATE _____

HOW TO USE A CULTURAL MAP

Apply Map and Globe Skills

DIRECTIONS: The map on page 216 of your textbook shows languages and religions of the Indian subcontinent today. Hinduism is the most practiced religion in India. The map at the right shows the distribution of Hindus in India shortly after India's independence. Use this map to answer the questions below.

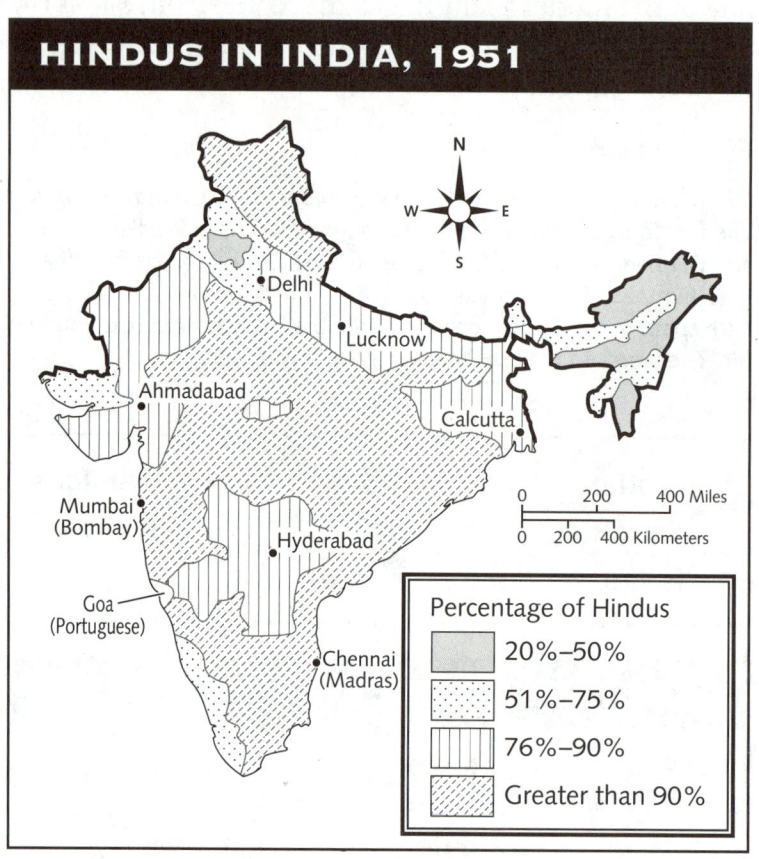

1. Which region of India had the lowest percentage of Hindus? **the northeast**

2. What percentage of the population was Hindu in the area surrounding Chennai?
   greater than 90%

3. In 1951 what was the name of the Portuguese possession on the west coast of India?
   Goa

4. What percentage of the population was Hindu in the area to the east of Goa?
   76%–90%

5. Did any parts of India have a population of less than 20% Hindu? How can you tell?
   no, because the lowest entry in the key begins with 20%

NAME _____ DATE _____

The Influence of Ashoka

Draw Conclusions

DIRECTIONS: Read the paragraphs on this page. Use this information and your textbook to answer the questions that follow.

The Wheel of Ashoka is shown on the flag of India. This wheel design was carved on the stone pillars that proclaimed the edicts of the emperor Ashoka. The Wheel of Ashoka represents law.

To spread his law, Ashoka sent his son Mahendra to lead a group of Buddhist missionaries to the nearby island of Ceylon (present-day Sri Lanka). The king of Ceylon, his court, and most of the people converted to Buddhism. Sri Lanka is still mostly Buddhist.

1. The wheel and the lion, two designs used by Ashoka, are symbols of modern India. Why do you think Ashoka is honored in India today? *Ashoka is remembered and honored because he used his authority to better the lives of his people.*

2. Would you say that Mahendra was more like his father, Ashoka, or his great-grandfather, Chandragupta? Explain your answer. *Mahendra was more like Ashoka, who lived according to the peaceful ways of Buddhism. Chandragupta was cruel and brutal.*

3. In what way did the island kingdom of Ceylon follow Ashoka more closely than did Ashoka's own country of India? *After Ashoka's death many of his ideas were forgotten and Buddhism faded away in India. Buddhism has continued to flourish in Sri Lanka.*

4. Based on what you have learned about the Maurya Empire in India, what are two ways a ruler can unite the people of a country? Which do you think is the better way? Explain your answer. *A ruler can unite people by force or by fairness. Accept answers that the students can support.*

Use after reading Chapter 5, Lesson 4, pages 218–223.

NAME _____ DATE _____

MILITARY Technology

Make Comparisons

DIRECTIONS: Read the two "news reports" below. Then look at the military technology listed in the box on the next page. Write the name of each item in the correct column, according to the army that used it. Some items might have been used by both armies.

CYRUS CONQUERS PERSIA

PERSIA—Cyrus the Great has overpowered kingdoms from the Indus River to beyond the Nile. A smart strategist, Cyrus knows how to use the great number of soldiers at his command. His conquest of Babylon has freed the Jews held captive there, and he has allowed them to return to their own land. Their prophet Isaiah has written that Cyrus "tramples kings under foot; he makes them like dust with his sword, like driven stubble with his bow." The historian Herodotus credits Cyrus's success to his growing up in a tribe of tough herdsmen and horsemen. "Soft countries breed soft men," he commented. Cyrus and his followers "chose to live in a rugged land and rule rather than to cultivate rich plains and be slaves."

UN FORCES WIN IN GULF

PERSIAN GULF—Just before dawn on August 2, 1990, Iraq took control of the much smaller country of Kuwait. The U.S. and 27 other countries condemned the invasion and demanded that Iraq withdraw. Saddam Hussein, president of Iraq, refused. Most other nations cut off trade with Iraq. Hussein declared that Kuwait was now part of Iraq. In November the U.S. powered up for war by sending troops, tanks, aircraft, and ships to the Persian Gulf area. The United Nations Security Council gave Iraq a deadline for withdrawal. Negotiations continued. On January 17, 1991, U.S. and allied forces fought back. Their high-tech weaponry stunned Iraq. On February 27 Kuwait was liberated, and a cease-fire was declared.

(Continued)

NAME _____ DATE _____

MILITARY TECHNOLOGY OF THE TIME

tanks	horses
swords	soldiers
aircraft	bows and arrows
ships	

CYRUS THE GREAT'S ARMY	UNITED NATIONS FORCES
swords	tanks
horses	aircraft
soldiers	ships
bows and arrows	soldiers

Use after reading Chapter 5, Lesson 5, pages 224–227.

NAME _____ DATE _____

INDIA AND PERSIA

Connect Main Ideas

DIRECTIONS: Use this organizer to describe the cultures of ancient India and Persia. List three details to support each main idea listed below.

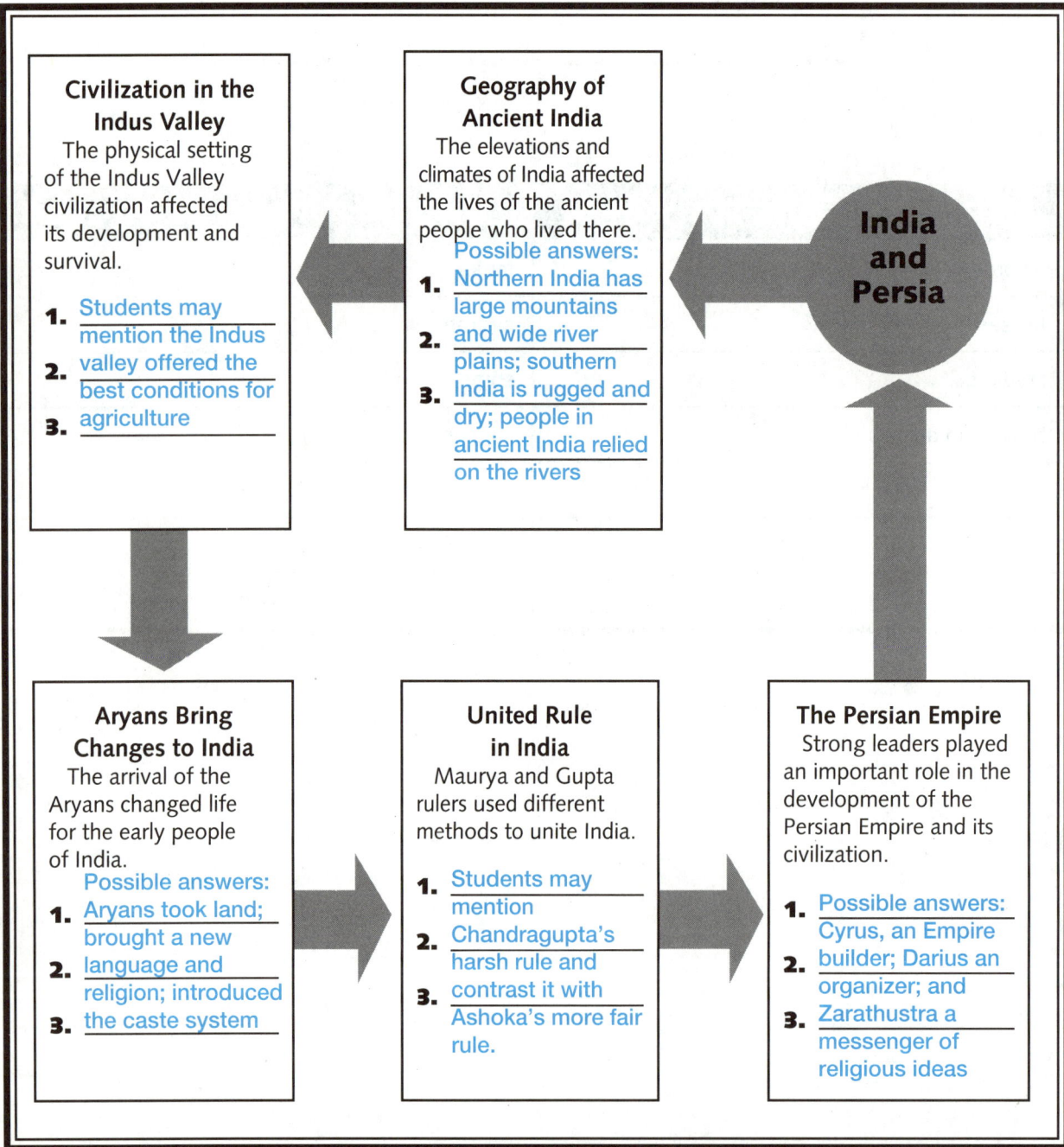

Civilization in the Indus Valley
The physical setting of the Indus Valley civilization affected its development and survival.
1. Students may mention the Indus
2. valley offered the best conditions for
3. agriculture

Geography of Ancient India
The elevations and climates of India affected the lives of the ancient people who lived there.
Possible answers:
1. Northern India has large mountains
2. and wide river plains; southern
3. India is rugged and dry; people in ancient India relied on the rivers

Aryans Bring Changes to India
The arrival of the Aryans changed life for the early people of India.
Possible answers:
1. Aryans took land; brought a new
2. language and religion; introduced
3. the caste system

United Rule in India
Maurya and Gupta rulers used different methods to unite India.
1. Students may mention
2. Chandragupta's harsh rule and
3. contrast it with Ashoka's more fair rule.

The Persian Empire
Strong leaders played an important role in the development of the Persian Empire and its civilization.
1. Possible answers: Cyrus, an Empire
2. builder; Darius an organizer; and
3. Zarathustra a messenger of religious ideas

46 ACTIVITY BOOK   Use after reading Chapter 5, pages 198–229.

NAME _____ DATE _____

INDIA AND PERSIA

Connect Main Ideas

DIRECTIONS: Use this organizer to describe the cultures of ancient India and Persia. List three details to support each main idea listed below.

Civilization in the Indus Valley
The physical setting of the Indus Valley civilization affected its development and survival.
1. Students may mention the Indus
2. valley offered the best conditions for
3. agriculture

Geography of Ancient India
The elevations and climates of India affected the lives of the ancient people who lived there.
Possible answers:
1. Northern India has large mountains
2. and wide river plains; southern
3. India is rugged and dry; people in ancient India relied on the rivers

India and Persia

Aryans Bring Changes to India
The arrival of the Aryans changed life for the early people of India.
Possible answers:
1. Aryans took land; brought a new
2. language and religion; introduced
3. the caste system

United Rule in India
Maurya and Gupta rulers used different methods to unite India.
1. Students may mention
2. Chandragupta's harsh rule and
3. contrast it with Ashoka's more fair rule.

The Persian Empire
Strong leaders played an important role in the development of the Persian Empire and its civilization.
1. Possible answers: Cyrus, an Empire builder; Darius an
2. organizer; and
3. Zarathustra a messenger of religious ideas

46 ACTIVITY BOOK   Use after reading Chapter 5, pages 198–229.

NAME _____ DATE _____

MILITARY TECHNOLOGY OF THE TIME

tanks	horses
swords	soldiers
aircraft	bows and arrows
ships	

CYRUS THE GREAT'S ARMY	UNITED NATIONS FORCES
swords	tanks
horses	aircraft
soldiers	ships
bows and arrows	soldiers

Use after reading Chapter 5, Lesson 5, pages 224–227.

NAME _____ DATE _____

MILITARY
Technology

Make Comparisons

DIRECTIONS: Read the two "news reports" below. Then look at the military technology listed in the box on the next page. Write the name of each item in the correct column, according to the army that used it. Some items might have been used by both armies.

CYRUS CONQUERS PERSIA

PERSIA—Cyrus the Great has overpowered kingdoms from the Indus River to beyond the Nile. A smart strategist, Cyrus knows how to use the great number of soldiers at his command. His conquest of Babylon has freed the Jews held captive there, and he has allowed them to return to their own land. Their prophet Isaiah has written that Cyrus "tramples kings under foot; he makes them like dust with his sword, like driven stubble with his bow." The historian Herodotus credits Cyrus's success to his growing up in a tribe of tough herdsmen and horsemen. "Soft countries breed soft men," he commented. Cyrus and his followers "chose to live in a rugged land and rule rather than to cultivate rich plains and be slaves."

UN FORCES WIN IN GULF

PERSIAN GULF—Just before dawn on August 2, 1990, Iraq took control of the much smaller country of Kuwait. The U.S. and 27 other countries condemned the invasion and demanded that Iraq withdraw. Saddam Hussein, president of Iraq, refused. Most other nations cut off trade with Iraq. Hussein declared that Kuwait was now part of Iraq. In November the U.S. powered up for war by sending troops, tanks, aircraft, and ships to the Persian Gulf area. The United Nations Security Council gave Iraq a deadline for withdrawal. Negotiations continued. On January 17, 1991, U.S. and allied forces fought back. Their high-tech weaponry stunned Iraq. On February 27 Kuwait was liberated, and a cease-fire was declared.

(Continued)

44 ACTIVITY BOOK

Use after reading Chapter 5, Lesson 5, pages 224–227.

NAME _____ DATE _____

The Influence of Ashoka

Draw Conclusions

DIRECTIONS: Read the paragraphs on this page. Use this information and your textbook to answer the questions that follow.

    The Wheel of Ashoka is shown on the flag of India. This wheel design was carved on the stone pillars that proclaimed the edicts of the emperor Ashoka. The Wheel of Ashoka represents law.

    To spread his law, Ashoka sent his son Mahendra to lead a group of Buddhist missionaries to the nearby island of Ceylon (present-day Sri Lanka). The king of Ceylon, his court, and most of the people converted to Buddhism. Sri Lanka is still mostly Buddhist.

1. The wheel and the lion, two designs used by Ashoka, are symbols of modern India. Why do you think Ashoka is honored in India today? *Ashoka is remembered and honored because he used his authority to better the lives of his people.*

2. Would you say that Mahendra was more like his father, Ashoka, or his great-grandfather, Chandragupta? Explain your answer. *Mahendra was more like Ashoka, who lived according to the peaceful ways of Buddhism. Chandragupta was cruel and brutal.*

3. In what way did the island kingdom of Ceylon follow Ashoka more closely than did Ashoka's own country of India? *After Ashoka's death many of his ideas were forgotten and Buddhism faded away in India. Buddhism has continued to flourish in Sri Lanka.*

4. Based on what you have learned about the Maurya Empire in India, what are two ways a ruler can unite the people of a country? Which do you think is the better way? Explain your answer. *A ruler can unite people by force or by fairness. Accept answers that the students can support.*

Use after reading Chapter 5, Lesson 4, pages 218–223.

HOW TO USE A CULTURAL MAP

Apply Map and Globe Skills

DIRECTIONS: The map on page 216 of your textbook shows languages and religions of the Indian subcontinent today. Hinduism is the most practiced religion in India. The map at the right shows the distribution of Hindus in India shortly after India's independence. Use this map to answer the questions below.

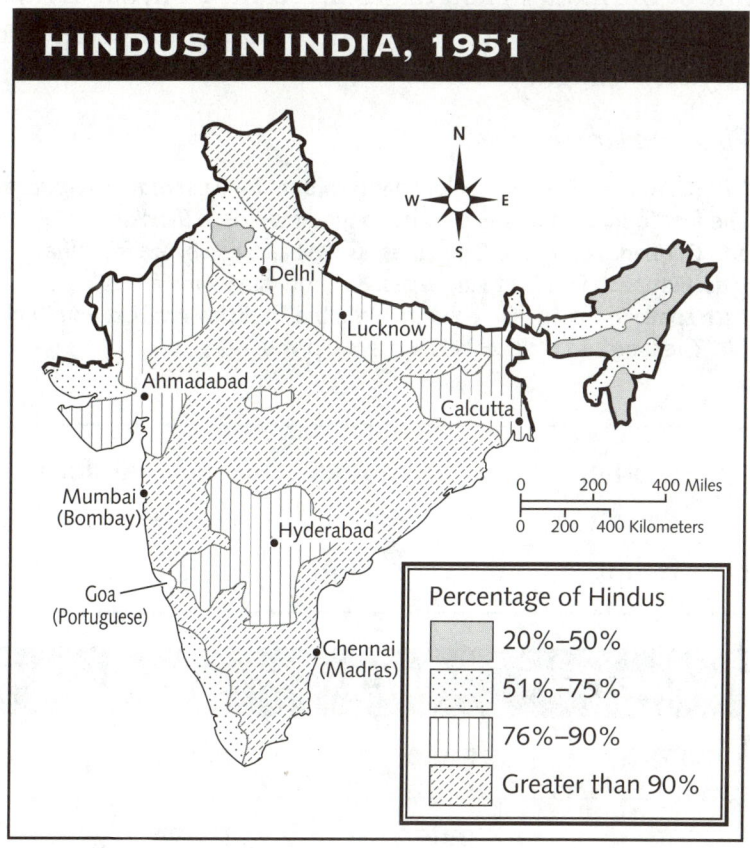

1. Which region of India had the lowest percentage of Hindus? **the northeast**

2. What percentage of the population was Hindu in the area surrounding Chennai?
greater than 90%

3. In 1951 what was the name of the Portuguese possession on the west coast of India?
Goa

4. What percentage of the population was Hindu in the area to the east of Goa?
76%–90%

5. Did any parts of India have a population of less than 20% Hindu? How can you tell?
no, because the lowest entry in the key begins with 20%

A Family of Languages

Almost half the people in the world today speak an Indo-European language. English is an Indo-European language. So is Hindi, which is spoken by many people in India. Hindi is one of the modern languages that came from Sanskrit, the ancient language that one group of Indo-Europeans, the Aryans, brought to India.

Find Similarities

DIRECTIONS: The table below has a column for each of five languages. The first four columns show some common words in Sanskrit, Greek, Latin, and German. These four languages, as well as English, are from the Indo-European family of languages. See how the words are alike. In each space in the English column, write the English word that you think fits. The words in the box below may help you.

brother	mother	sister
daughter	new	three
father	seven	

SANSKRIT	GREEK	LATIN	GERMAN	ENGLISH
matar	meter	mater	mutter	mother
pitar	pater	pater	vater	father
bhratar	adelphos	frater	bruder	brother
svasar	adelphe	soror	schwester	sister
duhitar	thugater	filia	tochter	daughter
navos	neos	novus	neu	new
trayas	treis	tres	drei	three
sapta	hepta	septem	sieben	seven

Use after reading Chapter 5, Lesson 3, pages 210–215.

NAME _____ DATE _____

Life in the City

Archaeologists first excavated the Harappan cities of the Indus Valley in the 1920s and 1930s. Walled cities, about 3 miles (5 km) in diameter, contained government buildings, a huge grain shed on a raised upper level, and wide streets laid out in squares. Life in Harappan cities was well advanced for its time.

Make Observations

DIRECTIONS: This drawing shows how a house in a Harappan city may have looked. Study the picture. Recall what you have read in your text about Harappan architecture. Then answer the questions below.

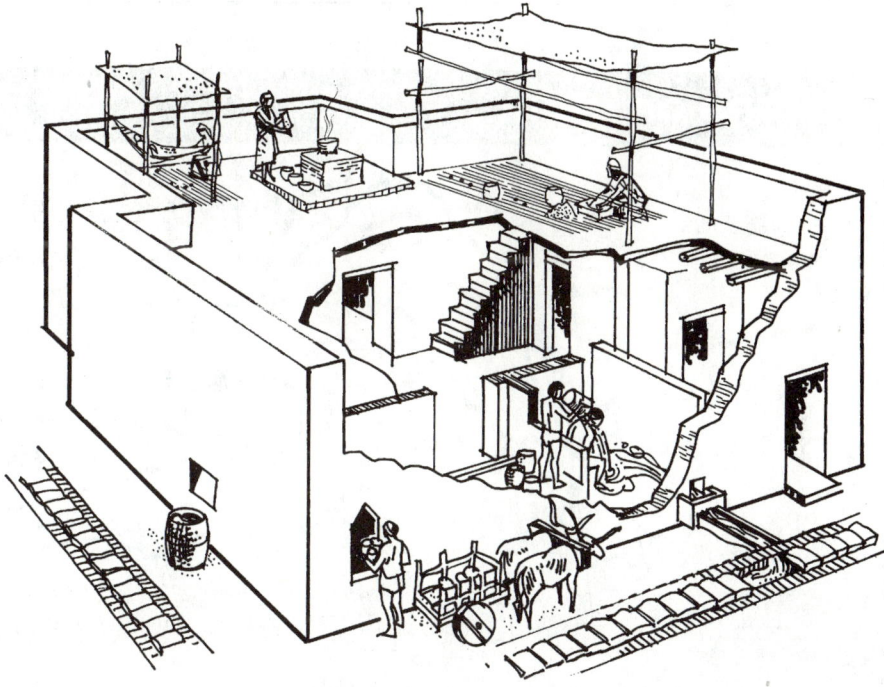

1. What "modern" conveniences do you see? <u>drains for water from bathroom, covered sewers in the street, chute for garbage</u>

2. Thick brick walls without windows helped keep the house cool. Why do you think the house was built on an open courtyard? <u>for natural light and fresh air</u>

3. What other means of staying cool do you see? <u>bathing, awnings on the roof for shade, cooking on the roof</u>

40   ACTIVITY BOOK   Use after reading Chapter 5, Lesson 2, pages 204–209.

NAME _____ DATE _____

9. What dangers have rivers and monsoons presented to the people of India?
Floods have destroyed homes, sometimes entire villages, and changed the course of the rivers.

10. What is deforestation, and how does it affect the patterns of river flow?
Deforestation is the widespread cutting down of trees. This has led to larger and larger flooding. Without trees in place, the flooding washes away the top layer of soil.

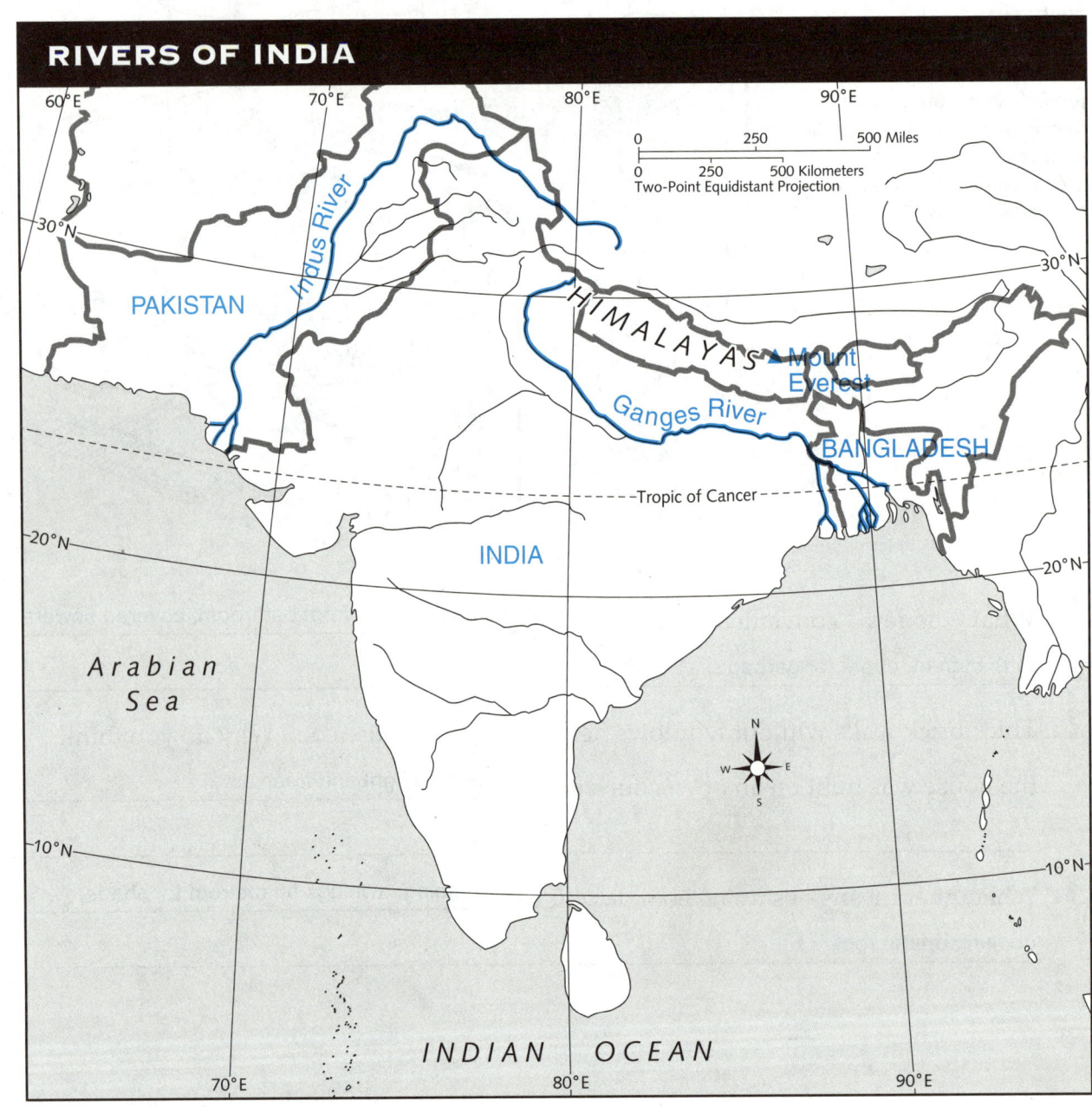

Use after reading Chapter 5, Lesson 1, pages 199–203.

NAME _____ DATE _____

Climate of China

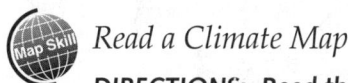 *Read a Climate Map*

DIRECTIONS: Read the paragraphs.

China's climate varies greatly from one region to another. You will recall that climate is the weather that a place has year after year. In many areas of China, winters are dry and summers are hot, rainy, and humid. However, there are regions where the climate is quite different.

In the north and northeast, summers are hot but dry, and winters last a long time and are very cold. In the desert regions of Xinjiang Uygur and Nei Monggol, or Inner Mongolia, summer is hot and dry while winter is cold and dry. North of the Chang Jiang, the winter temperatures can be extremely cold. In Beijing, there are occasional sandstorms in both winter and spring.

Northern China is dry the entire year. The precipitation it does have occurs mainly in summer, with almost none in winter. The opposite is true in southern China where there is much rain throughout the year, with a little less than half of the annual rainfall occurring in summer. In southeastern China, the rainy season in summer is severe and with it comes many typhoons.

In the west, on the Plateau of Tibet, little rain falls through the year. The summers are short and warm, and the winters are very cold. Day and night temperatures vary greatly. In central China, summers are hot and humid, with a lot of rainfall especially in late summer.

(Continued)

NAME _____ DATE _____

DIRECTIONS: The climate map below shows the yearly precipitation in China. Use the map and information from the paragraphs you just read to answer the questions.

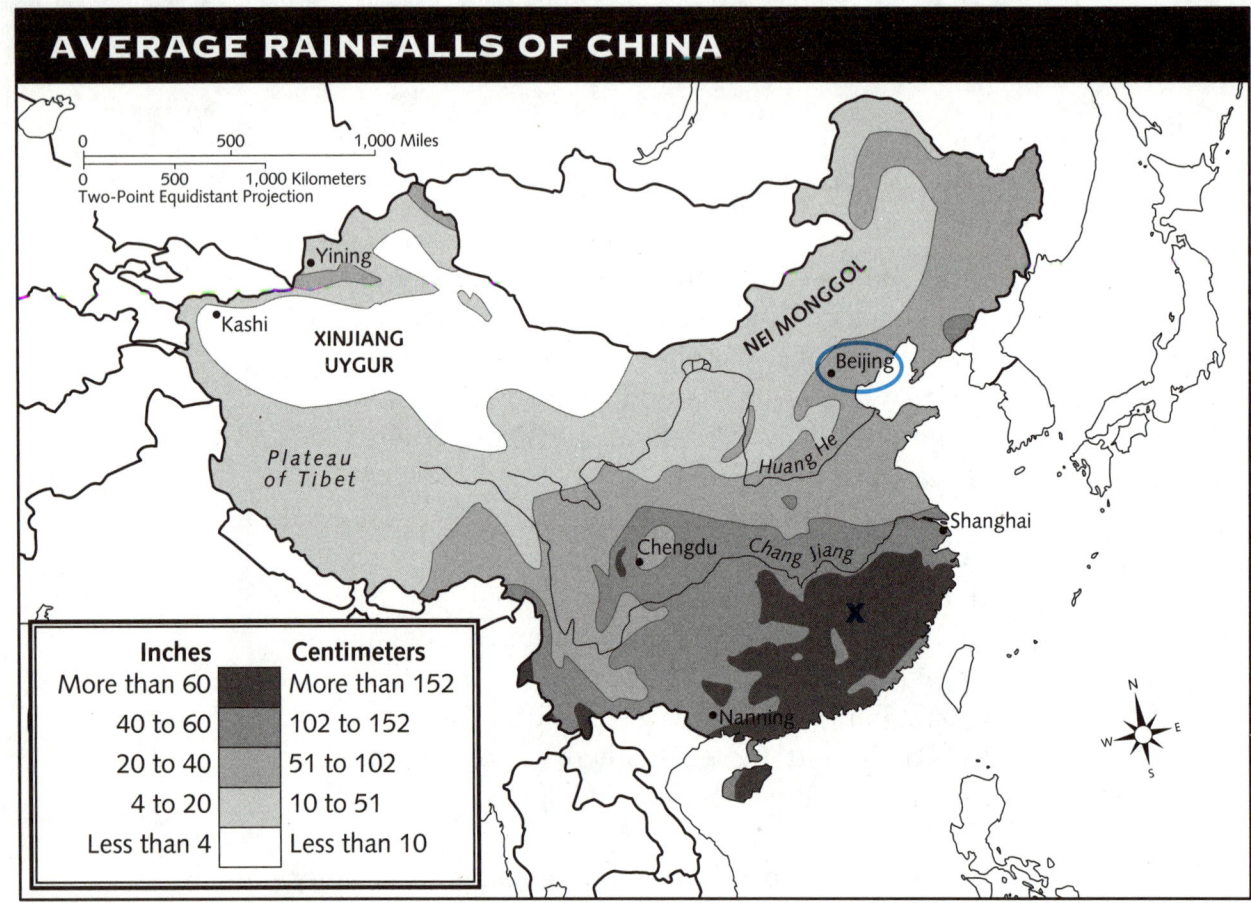

1. In which city could you expect to find sandstorms in spring? Beijing
   Circle the city on the map.

2. In which season do typhoons occur in southeastern China? summer
   Place an X on the map where many typhoons occur.

3. Which city has more rainfall, Shanghai or Beijing? Shanghai

4. If you visited Kashi, would you take a raincoat? Why or why not?
   No; there is little rain there.

5. Is the wettest part of China in the west or the east? east

NAME _____ DATE _____

In the Beginning

Use Source Material

DIRECTIONS: Read this Chinese myth. Then answer the questions that follow.

In the beginning the world was an enormous egg. Outside the egg was only darkness. Inside was only chaos—and a sleeping giant named Pan Gu. After a long time, Pan Gu woke up and cracked out of the eggshell. Part of the egg escaped and floated up to form the sky. The heavier part of the egg sank down and became the Earth. Pan Gu was worried that they might go back together, so he stood holding the Earth down with his giant feet and pushing the sky up with his arms. He kept the Earth and sky apart for thousands of years. Then Pan Gu lay down to die. Every part of Pan Gu was used to make the universe. His breath was turned into wind and clouds, and his voice into thunder. His left eye became the sun, his right eye became the moon, and his hair became the stars in the sky. His arms and legs grew into mountains, and his veins were roads and paths. Pan Gu's flesh turned into the soil in the fields, and his skin was the plants and trees. His bones and teeth were minerals buried in the earth, and his sweat became dew and rain. The fleas on the body of the giant Pan Gu became the first people.

1. According to Chinese mythology, what did Pan Gu give the Chinese people?
He gave them everything they needed to live in the universe.

2. Does the story of Pan Gu help you understand why the Chinese people believed their world was the center of the universe? Explain. Yes; it tells how the whole universe was created around them.

3. Do you think the story makes individuals seem important or unimportant? Explain.
It makes people seem unimportant, like fleas. Nature is bigger and more important.

4. How did the Chinese people think of their gods? as very powerful

Use after reading Chapter 6, Lesson 2, pages 235–241.

NAME _____ DATE _____

HOW TO USE ELEVATION MAPS

The land ruled by the Shang dynasty stretched more than 500 miles (805 km) along the Yellow Sea from north of the Huang He to just north of the Chang Jiang and inland about 1,000 miles (1609 km). Most of the Shang territory was low-lying, contrasting greatly with the hilly and mountainous regions that are part of China today.

Apply Map and Globe Skills

DIRECTIONS: The elevation below shows present-day China. Study the map and the elevation key. Then answer the questions on the next page.

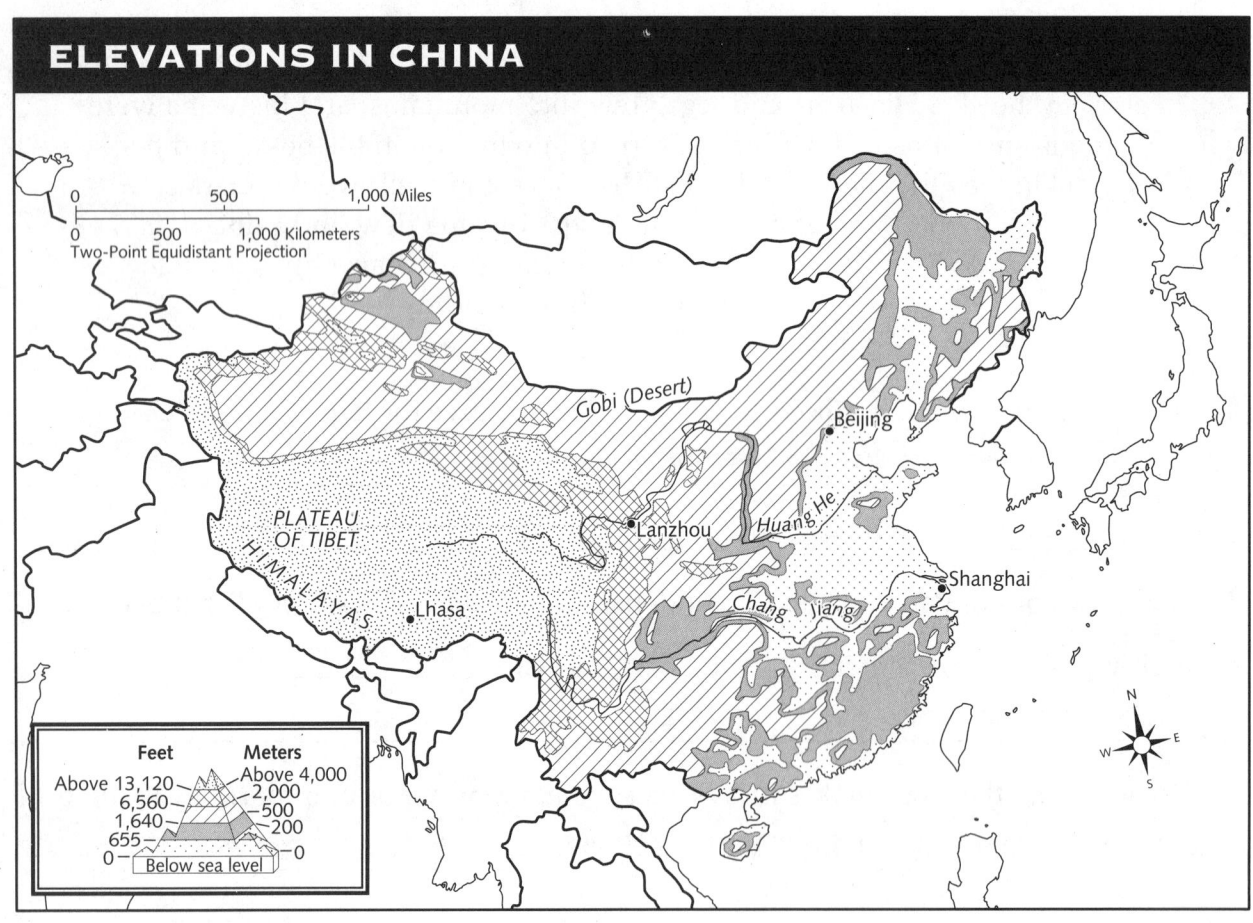

(Continued)

50 ACTIVITY BOOK   Use after reading Chapter 6, Skill Lesson, pages 242–243.

NAME _____   DATE _____

1. Find the present-day city of Beijing. In what elevation range does it lie?
   0–655 ft.

2. If you traveled from Shanghai to Beijing, would you be higher, lower, or at about the same elevation?
   at about the same elevation

3. Which city is higher, Beijing or Lanzhou?
   Lanzhou

4. Name the city that lies in the range of 13,120 feet or higher.
   Lhasa

5. What important physical feature is to the south of the Plateau of Tibet?
   the Himalayas

6. The Plateau of Tibet is sometimes called the "roof of the world." Why do you think this is so?
   because it is so high; because it is a very high plateau

7. Why do you think ancient Chinese cities were founded in the eastern low-lying areas, rather than in the west?
   It was easier to move to and from the low-lying places; it would have been easier to farm in lower ground than in mountainous regions.

8. The early Chinese kingdoms were often attacked from the north and northwest, rather than from the south and southwest. Why might that have been so?
   It was easier to travel southward from the north than across the mountains and elevated plateaus of the south and southwest.

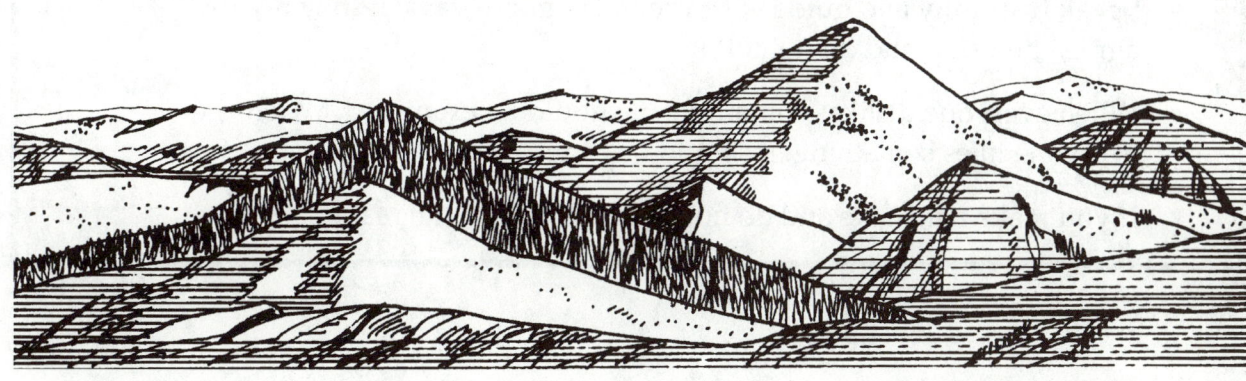

Use after reading Chapter 6, Skill Lesson, pages 242–243.

NAME _____ DATE _____

Confucius Said...

The followers of Confucius wrote down his teachings in the form of proverbs, or short sayings. His teachings became a guide for the way many people lived. The following sayings are based on the book known as the *Analects*.

Understand Ideas and Values

DIRECTIONS: Read the sayings of Confucius below. Then look at the sentences on page 53. Write whether Confucius would have agreed or disagreed with each statement. Explain your answer.

SOME SAYINGS OF CONFUCIUS

- Good people bring out what is good in others, not what is bad.

- To eat your fill but not apply your mind to anything all day is a problem. Are there no games to play? Even that would be smarter than doing nothing.

- People who do not think far enough ahead always have worries near at hand.

- Don't worry that no one recognizes you; seek to be worthy of recognition.

- Speak truthfully and guide your friends in good ways. If they do not agree, then stop and do not follow them.

- When everyone dislikes something, it should be examined. When everyone likes something, it should be examined.

- If you make a mistake and do not correct it, this is the real mistake.

(Continued)

NAME _____ DATE _____

1. It is all right for children to watch television all day during summer vacation. Confucius would have disagreed. They should look for something useful to do. They could read, study, or at least play a game.

2. You have an influence on your friends. Confucius would have agreed. You should set a good example and try to help your friends do what is right.

3. Follow the crowd. Confucius would have disagreed. You should examine, or look carefully at, what "everyone" likes or dislikes and then make your own decision.

4. Don't bother to plan ahead, because your plans usually will not work out. Confucius would have disagreed. If you don't make plans, you'll worry about what will happen.

5. Learn from your mistakes. Confucius would have agreed. The real mistake is in failing to improve.

6. Be sure that everyone knows who you are. Confucius would have disagreed. It is more important to be worthy of recognition than to have it.

NAME _____ DATE _____

HOW TO IDENTIFY CAUSES AND THEIR EFFECTS

Apply Critical Thinking Skills

DIRECTIONS: Read the pairs of statements about the ancient Chinese. Decide which is the cause and which is the effect. Indicate each by marking the statements with C (Cause) or E (Effect).

1. __C__ The ocean, desert, mountains, and plateau formed natural barriers.
   __E__ Ancient Chinese culture was able to develop without foreign invasion.

2. __E__ The Shang defeated the Xia.
   __C__ The Shang dynasty had metal weapons and chariots.

3. __E__ The Zhou benefited from achievements of the Shang.
   __C__ The Shang made use of bronze, chariots, and highly organized armies.

4. __C__ The Zhou worshipped a god called Tian, or "Heaven," and believed in the Mandate of Heaven.
   __E__ The Zhou became known as the Celestial Kingdom.

5. __E__ People today have an understanding of what happened during the Zhou dynasty.
   __C__ During the Zhou dynasty much was written about events that took place.

(Continued)

NAME _____ DATE _____

DIRECTIONS: *Sometimes effects become causes of other effects. Read the statements that follow. Then number them in the correct order that they occur as a series of causes and effects.*

__5__ Food supplies are increased.

__2__ Iron replaces bronze.

__3__ Iron is used for farming tools.

__6__ Population grows.

__4__ Agriculture is improved.

__1__ New metal technology is invented.

DIRECTIONS: *Retell the story of King You as a series of causes and effects. You may want to refer to your textbook for the details.*

King You sent out false alarms, which caused his armies to not believe his signals for help. This, in turn, caused them to fail to respond when he really needed their help, which, in turn, added to his weakness, contributed to his defeat and death, to the overall decline of the Zhou dynasty, and, in turn, to the time of the Warring Kingdoms Period.

Use after reading Chapter 6, Skill Lesson, pages 250–251.

ACTIVITY BOOK 55

NAME _____ DATE _____

A China Diary

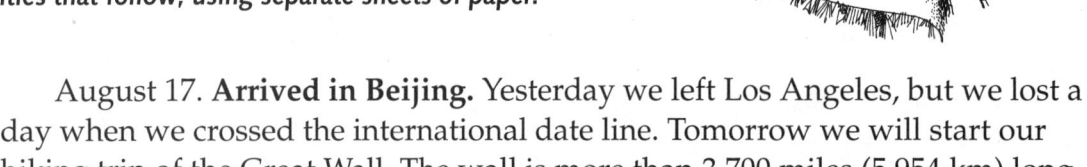

Apply Information

DIRECTIONS: Read the diary entries, which could have been written by a student vacationing in China. Then complete the activities that follow, using separate sheets of paper.

August 17. **Arrived in Beijing.** Yesterday we left Los Angeles, but we lost a day when we crossed the international date line. Tomorrow we will start our hiking trip of the Great Wall. The wall is more than 3,700 miles (5,954 km) long.

August 18. **BaDaLing.** Today we began our hike at the BaDaLing, or the North Pass. BaDaLing was the outpost that protected the capital from enemies. Some of this part of the wall was built with green bricks from the hills.

August 19. **BiShuShanZhuang.** What a day! We hiked to a Ming Tomb and toured BiShuShanZhuang, the summer palace. BiShuShanZhuang means "Mountain Home for Escaping the Summer Heat." This huge palace was started in 1703. Qing dynasty emperors spent about six months of the year here.

August 20. **JimShanLing.** Imagine! We passed 67 watchtowers along 7 miles (11.3 km), and each one looks completely different. We are told that this is the most spectacular sight of the whole Great Wall.

August 22. **HuangYaGuan.** At the city of BaGua we visited a museum, a Buddhist temple, and a maze park. Tomorrow we are going to QingDongLong. That is where hundreds of royals are buried.

August 24. **ShanHaiGuan.** We walked from JiaShan to ShanHaiGuan, the Old Dragon Head. It is the only part of the Great Wall that goes into the sea. We also saw the JiaShan Mountain. That is the mountain that the Great Wall climbs. And we saw JiuMenKou, the only part of the wall shaped like a bridge.

August 25. **Beijing.** We have returned to the capital again. Now we are resting a day before we see other sights.

1. Draw a map that shows the student's route.

2. Write a paragraph that explains which part of the trip interests you the most and tell why.

(Continued)

A China Diary

Apply Information

DIRECTIONS: Read the diary entries, which could have been written by a student vacationing in China. Then complete the activities that follow, using separate sheets of paper.

August 17. **Arrived in Beijing.** Yesterday we left Los Angeles, but we lost a day when we crossed the international date line. Tomorrow we will start our hiking trip of the Great Wall. The wall is more than 3,700 miles (5,954 km) long.

August 18. **BaDaLing.** Today we began our hike at the BaDaLing, or the North Pass. BaDaLing was the outpost that protected the capital from enemies. Some of this part of the wall was built with green bricks from the hills.

August 19. **BiShuShanZhuang.** What a day! We hiked to a Ming Tomb and toured BiShuShanZhuang, the summer palace. BiShuShanZhuang means "Mountain Home for Escaping the Summer Heat." This huge palace was started in 1703. Qing dynasty emperors spent about six months of the year here.

August 20. **JimShanLing.** Imagine! We passed 67 watchtowers along 7 miles (11.3 km), and each one looks completely different. We are told that this is the most spectacular sight of the whole Great Wall.

August 22. **HuangYaGuan.** At the city of BaGua we visited a museum, a Buddhist temple, and a maze park. Tomorrow we are going to QingDongLong. That is where hundreds of royals are buried.

August 24. **ShanHaiGuan.** We walked from JiaShan to ShanHaiGuan, the Old Dragon Head. It is the only part of the Great Wall that goes into the sea. We also saw the JiaShan Mountain. That is the mountain that the Great Wall climbs. And we saw JiuMenKou, the only part of the wall shaped like a bridge.

August 25. **Beijing.** We have returned to the capital again. Now we are resting a day before we see other sights.

1. Draw a map that shows the student's route.

2. Write a paragraph that explains which part of the trip interests you the most and tell why.

(Continued)

NAME _____ DATE _____

DIRECTIONS: Sometimes effects become causes of other effects. Read the statements that follow. Then number them in the correct order that they occur as a series of causes and effects.

___5___ Food supplies are increased.

___2___ Iron replaces bronze.

___3___ Iron is used for farming tools.

___6___ Population grows.

___4___ Agriculture is improved.

___1___ New metal technology is invented.

DIRECTIONS: Retell the story of King You as a series of causes and effects. You may want to refer to your textbook for the details.

King You sent out false alarms, which caused his armies to not believe his signals for help. This, in turn, caused them to fail to respond when he really needed their help, which, in turn, added to his weakness, contributed to his defeat and death, to the overall decline of the Zhou dynasty, and, in turn, to the time of the Warring Kingdoms Period.

NAME _____ DATE _____

DIRECTIONS: Read the selection and answer the questions.

    In the distant past, perhaps around the fifth century B.C., rulers of small, independent kingdoms in northern China built walls. They wished to protect their kingdoms from one another and from nomads that sometimes attacked from the north. In 221 B.C. the emperor Shi Huangdi, who united China, linked together the separate walls. He ordered that the northern walls be connected to form a single line of defense. All available material was used: clay, stone, willow branches, reeds, and sand. After seven years, Shi Huangdi's Great Wall stretched for almost 1,500 miles (2,414 km) across northern China. Later, other emperors extended and strengthened the wall. During the Ming dynasty (A.D. 1368–1644) the wall was repaired and parts of it were rebuilt. In many places brick and stone slabs replaced the clay and earth. The Great Wall became a symbol of a strong empire.

1. How is the Great Wall a symbol of Shi Huangdi's great empire?
The wall's size and strength are symbols of the increasing size and power of the united empire of Shi Huangdi.

2. How does the building of the Great Wall illustrate Shi Huangdi's style of governing? Shi Huangdi brought China together — he united the separate walls into one wall.

3. Why was the Great Wall first built along the northern border of China?
The wall was built in the north to protect China from invaders from the north.

4. Why do you think the wall has lasted for so long? The wall is a great symbol for China and has been protected and repaired through the years; it was built to last.

Use after reading Chapter 6, Lesson 4, pages 252–257.

NAME _____ DATE _____

ANCIENT CHINESE SOLDIERS

Compare Illustrations

DIRECTIONS: The clay warriors found buried in the tomb of Shi Huangdi, at Xi'an, were dressed differently according to rank. Use information from the pictures below to compare the appearance of a commander and an infantryman. Then write your comparisons in the space provided.

COMMANDER	INFANTRYMAN
Students should point out that the commander is wearing armor, has a fancy headdress, and stands taller than the soldier.	Students should point out that the infantryman is not wearing armor or a fancy headdress; students may point out that the infantryman's arms appear to be in a martial art position.

COMMANDER

INFANTRYMAN

NAME _____   DATE _____

THE HAN HERITAGE

The period of the Han dynasty was a time of peace, wealth, and progress. It is sometimes called the Golden Age of China because many branches of arts and learning blossomed.

Organize Information

DIRECTIONS: Each oval in the web below describes an invention or advance made during the Han dynasty. Match each invention or advance with the area or field of knowledge shown below.

| government | language | trade | history | philosophy | technology |

Confucianism became official teaching; Daoism was also supported.
philosophy

Ambassadors were sent to make peace; civil service was established.
government

Seismograph was developed.
technology

Many traders traveled along the Silk Road.
trade

Paper was introduced; first Chinese dictionary was written.
language

Sima Qian recorded China's past.
history

Use after reading Chapter 6, Lesson 6, pages 262–267.

ACTIVITY BOOK 59

NAME _____ DATE _____

HOW TO CLASSIFY INFORMATION

Apply Chart and Graph Skills

DIRECTIONS: Review the list of words below. Then place the words into five different groups, or classifications. Write an appropriate heading for each classification.

Africa	Europe	Legalism	Sima Qian
apricots	Gaozu	Mediterranean Sea	wool
central Asia	gold	Qin dynasty	Wu Di
Chang'an	Han dynasty	Shang dynasty	Zhou dynasty
China	iron	Shi Huangdi	
Confucianism	ivory	silk	

Possible heading, GOODS
- apricots
- gold
- iron
- ivory
- silk
- wool

Possible heading, PEOPLE OF ANCIENT CHINA
- Gaozu
- Shi Huangdi
- Sima Qian
- Wu Di

Possible heading, DYNASTIES
- Han dynasty
- Qin dynasty
- Shang dynasty
- Zhou dynasty

Possible heading, PLACES
- Africa
- central Asia
- Chang'an
- China
- Europe
- Mediterranean Sea

Possible heading, PHILOSOPHIES
- Confucianism
- Legalism

Use after reading Chapter 6, Skill Lesson, pages 268–269.

NAME _____ DATE _____

CHINA

Connect Main Ideas

DIRECTIONS: Use this organizer to show that you understand the beginnings of Chinese civilization. Write a sentence or two that describes each topic listed below.

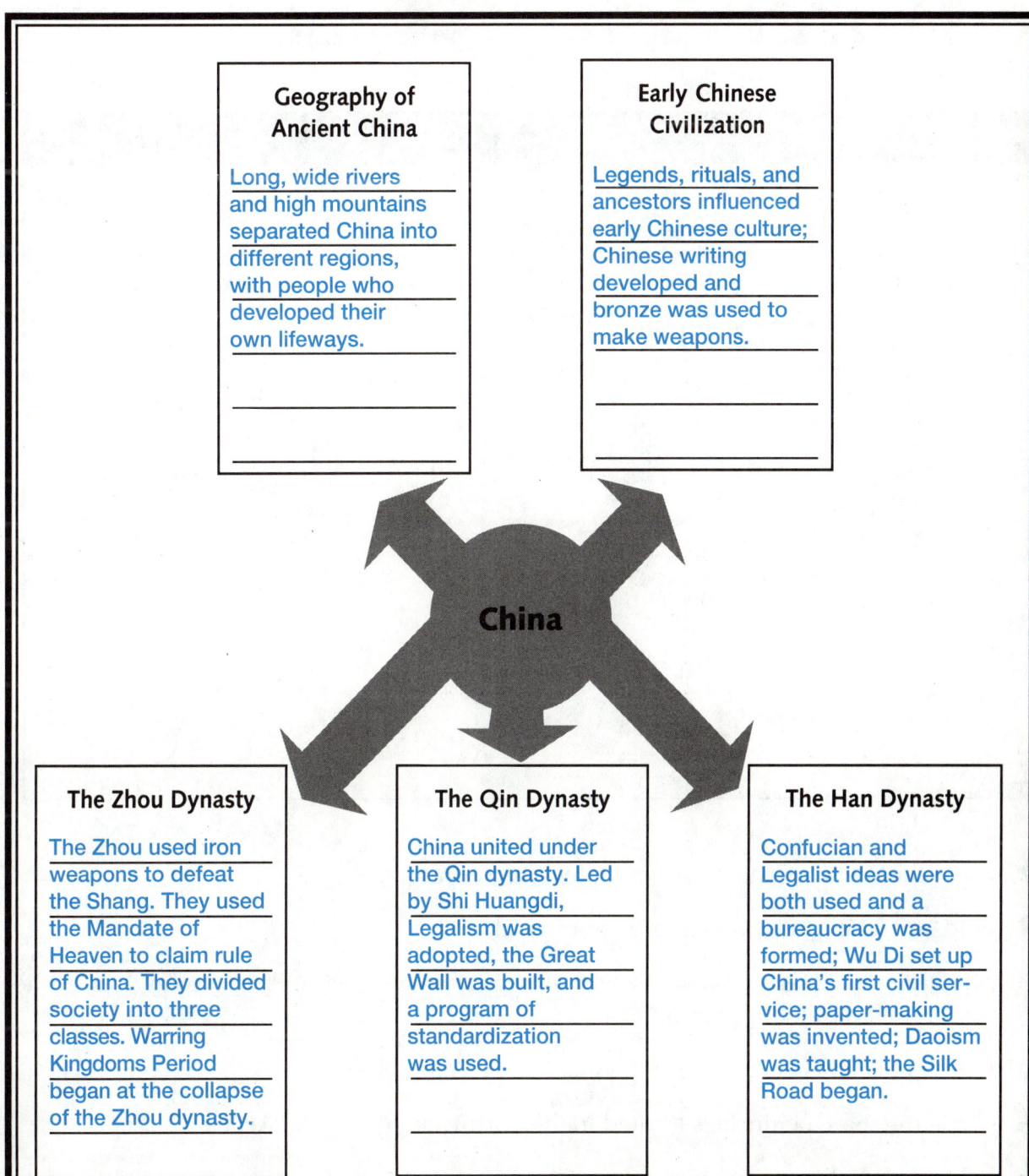

Geography of Ancient China

Long, wide rivers and high mountains separated China into different regions, with people who developed their own lifeways.

Early Chinese Civilization

Legends, rituals, and ancestors influenced early Chinese culture; Chinese writing developed and bronze was used to make weapons.

The Zhou Dynasty

The Zhou used iron weapons to defeat the Shang. They used the Mandate of Heaven to claim rule of China. They divided society into three classes. Warring Kingdoms Period began at the collapse of the Zhou dynasty.

The Qin Dynasty

China united under the Qin dynasty. Led by Shi Huangdi, Legalism was adopted, the Great Wall was built, and a program of standardization was used.

The Han Dynasty

Confucian and Legalist ideas were both used and a bureaucracy was formed; Wu Di set up China's first civil service; paper-making was invented; Daoism was taught; the Silk Road began.

Use after reading Chapter 6, pages 230–271.

NAME _____ DATE _____

A Nation of Islands, Peninsulas, & Water

Locate Features on a Map

DIRECTIONS: Greece is a nation of islands, peninsulas, and water. Use your textbook and the map below to complete the activities that follow.

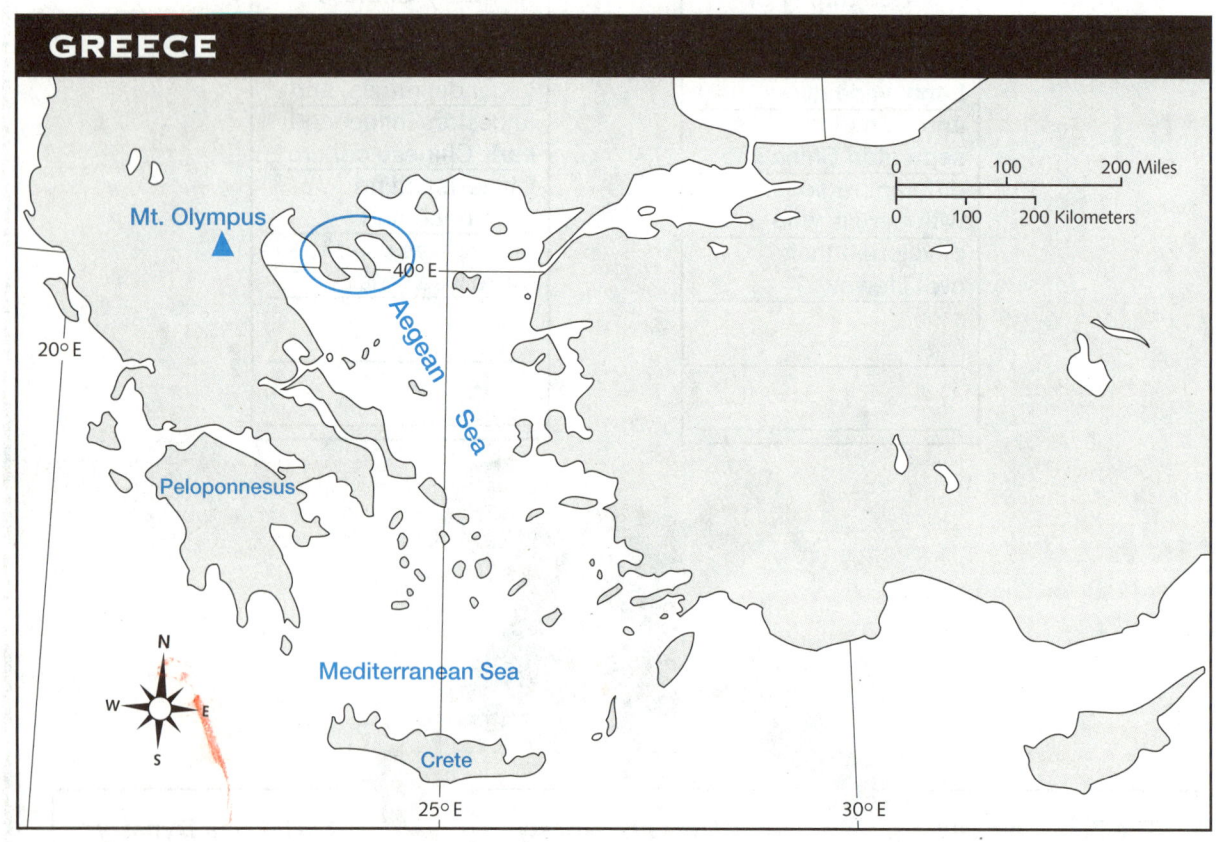

1. Label the Aegean Sea, which separates Greece from Turkey.

2. Find and label Crete, Greece's largest island.

3. Mt. Olympus is Greece's highest and most famous mountain. Place a triangle ▲ at the location of Mt. Olympus and label it.

4. Find and label Greece's largest peninsula, the Peloponnesus.

5. Circle the three peninsulas located in the northwest part of the Aegean Sea.

6. Label the Mediterranean Sea.

62 ACTIVITY BOOK   Use after reading Chapter 7, Lesson 1, pages 287–290.

NAME _____ DATE _____

Ancient Palaces of Crete

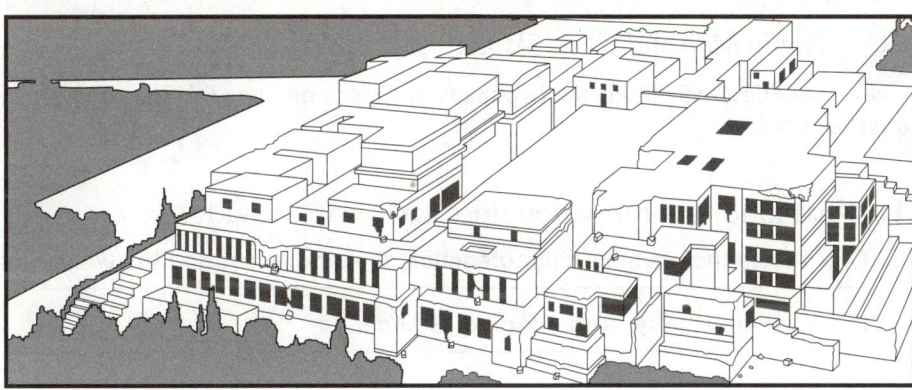

The Minoan palaces were built twice. The original palaces, built on hills around 1900 B.C., were destroyed by earthquakes around 1700 B.C. New palaces were built upon the ruins around 1650 B.C. They were mysteriously destroyed around 1400 B.C.

Read Information in a Table

DIRECTIONS: Read the information in the table, and answer the questions.

ANCIENT PALACES OF CRETE		
SITE	SIZE	FAST FACTS
Knossos	185 acres	King Minos's palace was made up of an elaborate maze of doorways, corridors, and staircases. This maze inspired the Greek myth of Daedalus and Icarus.
Malia	2 acres	This two-story tall palace was third in size and the most ordinary in design. Its houses and cemetery have been uncovered.
Phaistos	4.5 acres	This was the palace of King Minos's mythical brother, Radamanthys. This site shows how the new palace was built upon the old palace.
Zakros	less than 2 acres	This smallest of all the palaces was located on the sea. Its treasury room was the only one among the Minoan palaces that had not been robbed at some point.

1. At which site are there ruins of both the older and newer palaces? **Phaistos**
2. At which site was the smallest of the palaces? **Zakros**
3. Which site had the most ordinary design? **Malia**
4. Which site had a treasury that was not robbed? **Zakros**
5. Which site had an elaborate maze? **Knossos**

Use after reading Chapter 7, Lesson 2, pages 291–297.

NAME _____ DATE _____

HOW TO COMPARE Different Kinds of Maps

Apply Map and Globe Skills

DIRECTIONS: Study the two maps of Greece on page 65. Then answer the questions below.

1. What kind of information does each map provide?
   One shows the physical characteristics, the landforms, and the waterways of Greece; the other shows the major roads of Greece.

2. Which map would you use if you wanted to plan a trip from Athens to Corinth?
   the road map

3. In which direction would you travel on a trip from Athens to Corinth?
   west

4. Which map would you use if you were planning a boat trip on the seas and rivers of Greece?
   the physical map

5. What is the relationship between Greece's cities and mountains?
   The cities are not located on the mountains.

6. What is the relationship between the location of the roads and the mountains of Greece?
   There are few major roads in the mountains.

7. What do Athens, Patras, Thessalonica, and Corinth have in common?
   They are all on gulfs; they are all on the major road of Greece.

(Continued)

64 ACTIVITY BOOK — Use after reading Chapter 7, Skill Lesson, pages 298–299.

NAME _____ DATE _____

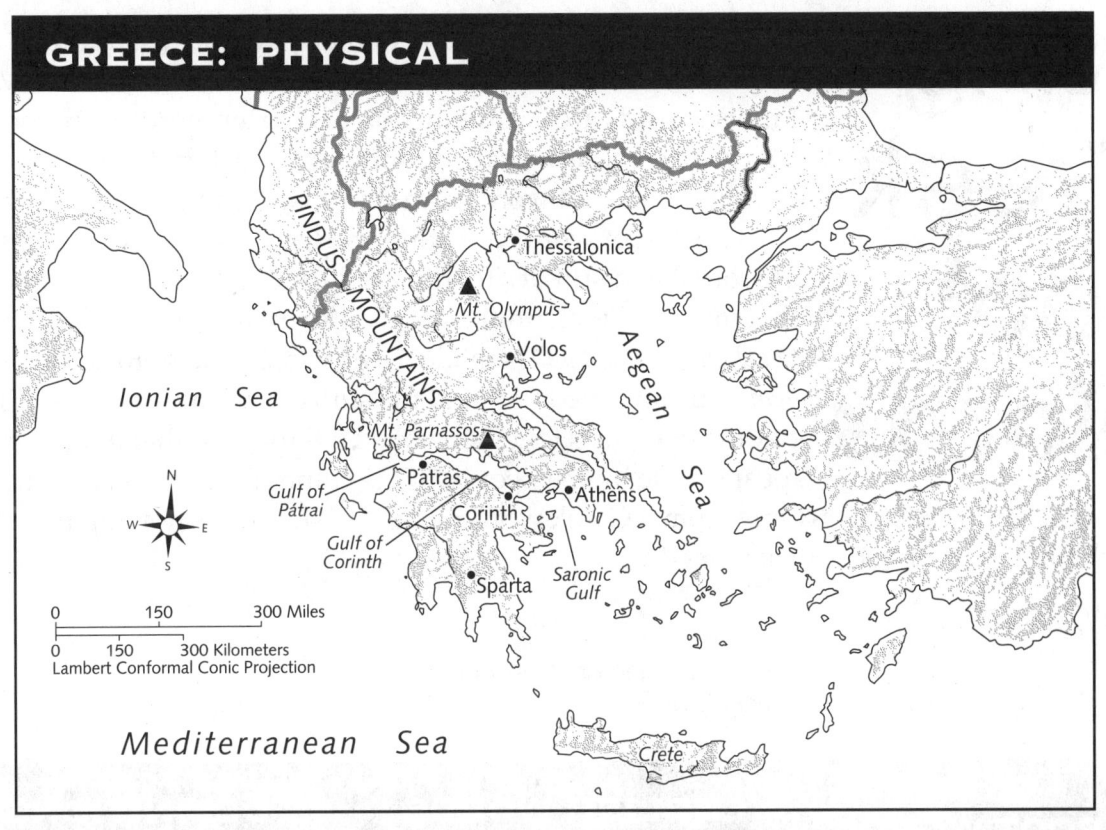

Use after reading Chapter 7, Skill Lesson, pages 298–299.

Using Greek Root Words

English is a combination of many languages. It contains words that come from French, German, Latin, and Greek. Many English words are a combination of shorter words from these languages. These are called **root words.** Just as the roots of a tree form its base, root words form the base for many English words.

Greek root words are often used as prefixes (beginnings of words) and suffixes (endings of words). Examples of words that include Greek prefixes and suffixes are *democracy* and *telephone. Democracy* is made up of two Greek words. The prefix *demos-* means "people," and the suffix *-cracy* means "rule." If you put the two parts together, you can figure out that *democracy* means "rule by the people." *Tele-* comes from a Greek word meaning "far," and *-phone* comes from a Greek word meaning "sound." Knowing this, do you think the telephone is well named?

Use Word Origins

DIRECTIONS: Use the Greek root words on the left to help you match the English words with their definitions.

GREEK ROOT WORDS	ENGLISH WORDS	DEFINITIONS
anti = against or opposite	1. __h__ antibiotic	a. a figure with five angles and five sides
athlon = athlete	2. __f__ bibliography	b. telling about a subject through pictures
biblio = book	3. __d__ chronometer	
bios = life	4. __c__ cryptograph	c. a secret written message
chronos = time	5. __i__ decathlon	d. an instrument for measuring time
crypt = secret or hidden	6. __j__ geology	e. the study of life
deca = ten	7. __b__ iconography	f. a list of books
geo = earth	8. __e__ biology	g. an instrument used to measure heat
gon = having many angles	9. __a__ pentagon	h. something that prevents or destroys life
graphy = writing	10. __g__ thermometer	i. a ten-event athletic contest
icon = image		
logy = study of		j. the study of the Earth
meter = measure		
penta = five		
thermos = heat		

NAME _____ DATE _____

What's Holding It Up?

Interpret Diagrams

DIRECTIONS: In classical Greek architecture, the first columns were designed in the Doric style. Then came the Ionic, followed by the Corinthian style. Study the diagrams and answer the questions that follow.

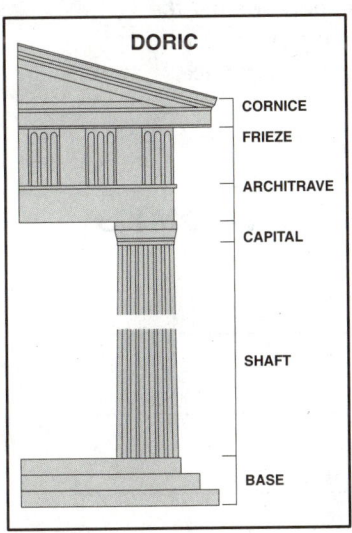
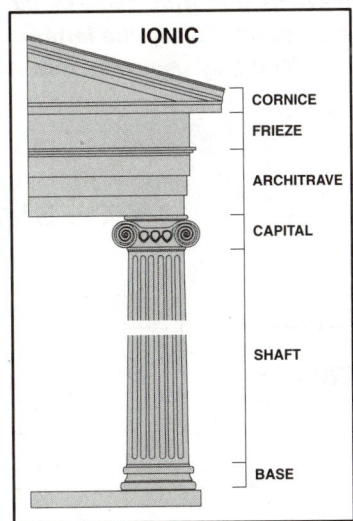
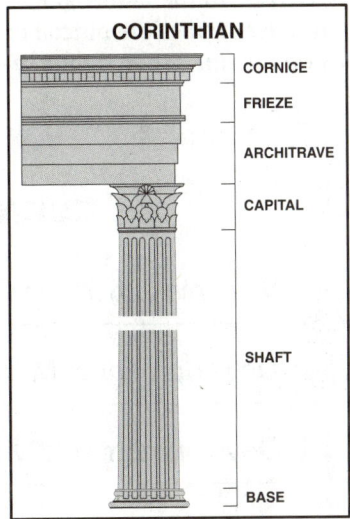

1. Which style has the fanciest capital? <u>Corinthian</u>
2. Which style has the plainest capital? <u>Doric</u>
3. What parts are common to all three styles? <u>shaft, capital, architrave, frieze, cornice</u>

4. What do you think is the purpose of the Greek columns?
   <u>Possible response: purpose is to bear the weight of what comes above; to hold up the architrave, frieze, and cornice; and to hold up the roof.</u>

5. What is the name of a building with Greek columns in your community?
   <u>Students' responses will vary.</u>

6. What style are the columns of the building in your answer to question 5?
   <u>Students' responses should reflect answers to Question 5.</u>

Use after reading Chapter 7, Lesson 4, pages 307–313.

NAME _____   DATE _____

HOW TO PREDICT LIKELY OUTCOMES

Apply Critical Thinking Skills

DIRECTIONS: In the table below are five events that took place in ancient Greece. Below the table is a list of possible outcomes for these events. Write the letter of the appropriate outcomes on the line at the right of each event. You may use some outcomes more than once.

EVENT	POSSIBLE OUTCOMES
Volcanic activity on Crete	b, g
Development of Minoan trade	a, e, h
Development of city-states	c, d, e, f, h
Greek victory in Persian Wars	b, e, i
Olympic Games	a, i

a. sharing of customs

b. destruction of property

c. rise of various forms of government

d. establishment of colonies

e. extension of Greek culture

f. development of political rivalries

g. destruction of historical records

h. spread of technology, language, and religion

i. development of Greek unity

ALEXANDER THE GREAT
Learns to Sword-Fight

By his death in 323 B.C., Alexander the Great had created one of the world's largest empires. Although the military tactics that he developed are more than 2,000 years old, they are still taught at military colleges around the world. At an early age, Alexander learned the skills a soldier of his time needed, including how to ride a horse, shoot a bow, and throw a spear.

Read a Biography

DIRECTIONS: A biographer is someone who writes about someone else's life. Alexander's most famous present-day biographer is Harold Lamb. The selection that follows is from Harold Lamb's book, *Alexander of Macedon: The Journey to World's End.* In the following selection, Alexander and his classmate Ptolemy are practicing their sword-fighting in front of their instructor. Read the selection, and answer the questions that follow.

"But Ptolemy fought viciously, carefully, easily managing to keep ahead of Alexander in the count of blows scored on the wooden shield. Clearly he showed that he was superior [to Alexander] in skill. Then, at times, he hurt Alexander . . . flicking the sword blade suddenly against his thigh or the side of his head, to draw blood and induce the [instructor] to stop the fight. Then Ptolemy would smile, as if tired of playing with such toys.

"Once the [instructor] had not stopped the sword-fight between the boys, and Alexander found himself limping so that he could barely shift his weight from one foot to the other, and blood running into his eyes half blinded him. He tried to shake the blood clear of his eyes; instead Ptolemy's face shone through a red haze, and suddenly the coldness went out of Alexander. His sword felt light, his arm moved free, and his legs drove him forward. Behind the red veil Ptolemy's shield was breaking, and his sword wavered helplessly.

"Alexander felt the fierce warmth of a headlong hunt, when he pressed close upon a weakened deer. Then he heard the [instructor] shouting, 'Rest!' and [the instructor's] spear knocked the swords apart. Ptolemy was sobbing and staggering about, badly hurt.

"The [instructor] held fast to Alexander's right arm and walked him away, until he quieted. 'If you can't master that temper,' he growled, 'you won't live long.'

"To Philip [Alexander's father] the [instructor] made a different report. 'He is incredibly fast, and he is much more dangerous than the others. But . . . he loses his head. I doubt if he will ever learn to use weapons as he should.'"

(Continued)

NAME _____ DATE _____

1. Do you think Alexander and Ptolemy were good friends? Explain your answer.
   no; because they fought against each other so viciously

2. What do you think is meant by the phrases "Ptolemy's face shone through a red haze" and "Behind the red veil"? that Alexander was looking through the blood covering his eyes

3. What do you think is meant by the phrase "and suddenly the coldness went out of Alexander"? that he forgot about his pain and became more aggressive

4. Why do you think Ptolemy reminded Alexander of a weakened deer?
   Like a weakened deer, Ptolemy was ready to be overtaken.

5. Why do you think the instructor gave Alexander's father a different report from what he actually said to Alexander? He did not want Alexander to remember that he had won the match, but rather that he had lost his temper, and that in battle, that could cost him his life.

NAME _____ DATE _____

ANCIENT GREECE

Connect Main Ideas

DIRECTIONS: Use this organizer to describe the history of ancient Greece. Write two examples for each box.

Geography of Ancient Greece
The mountains and the sea affected ancient Greek culture and history.
1. Students should mention that the mountains in Greece made inland travel and trade difficult; and
2. that Greece's natural harbors allowed the ancient Greeks to travel and trade by sea.

Ancient Greece

Alexander's Great Empire
Alexander brought many changes to the people of Europe and Asia.
1. Students may mention the extent of Alexander's empire, the spread of Greek culture, and the
2. achievements of Hellenistic mathematicians, geographers, and scientists.

Early People of Greece
The Minoans and the Mycenaeans were among the early people who lived in what is now Greece.
1. Students may mention that the Minoans settled on Crete and the Mycenaeans settled in the southern part of Greece; and
2. that the Mycenaeans borrowed from the Minoan culture.

City-States and Greek Culture
The people of ancient Greece developed different ways of life.
1. Students' answers should include mention of Sparta and its emphasis on a military society and Athens
2. and its democracy.

The Golden Age of Athens
Periods of war and peace affected the ways of life of ancient Greeks.
1. Students may mention that the Persian wars brought Greeks together while the Peloponnesian War tore them apart. The
2. peace between the two wars offered Athens a time of great achievement.

Use after reading Chapter 7, pages 286–325.

Geography of Italy

Map Skill — *Interpret Information on a Map*

DIRECTIONS: Most of Italy is mountainous or hilly. Less than one-quarter of the country is flat. Study the map. Then answer the questions.

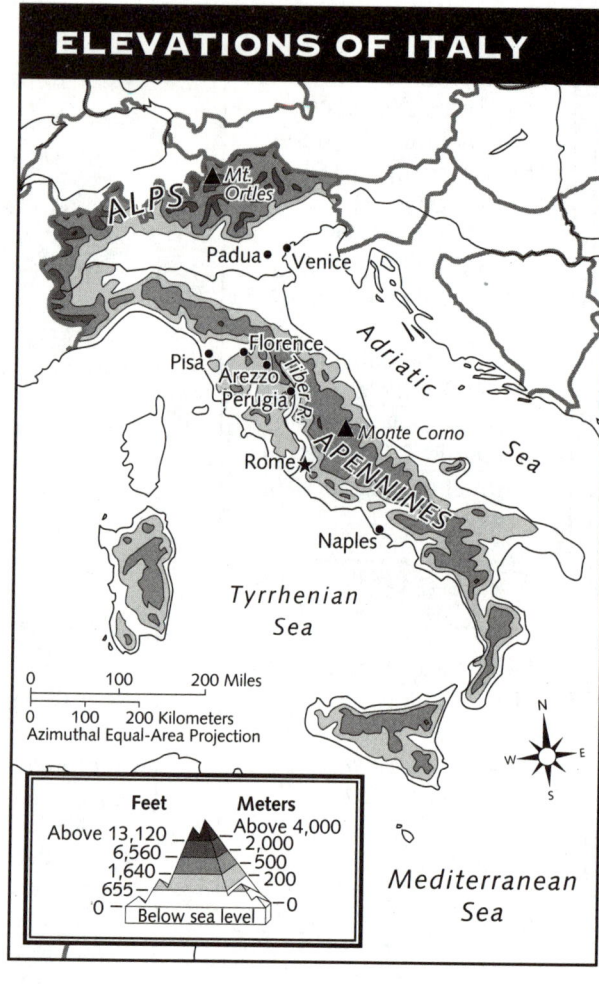

1. Which city is higher, Arezzo or Padua?

   Arezzo

2. How far is it from Monte Corno to the Adriatic Sea?

   about 30 miles (50 km)

3. What do Rome, Pisa, Naples, and Venice have in common?

   All are less than 655 feet (200 m) high;

   all are close to the sea.

4. In which direction would someone from Perugia travel to reach Italy's highest mountains?

   north

5. The Apennines have been called the spine of Italy. Why do you think this is so?

   The Apennines run lengthwise through the

   center of Italy, similar to the spine on a

   person's back.

NAME _____ DATE _____

ROMAN GOVERNMENT

Use an Organizational Chart

DIRECTIONS: In 753 B.C. Roman government began as a monarchy. By 494 B.C. Rome was a republic. The structure of that republic is shown below. Use your textbook to help you fill in the blanks in the chart and answer the questions that follow.

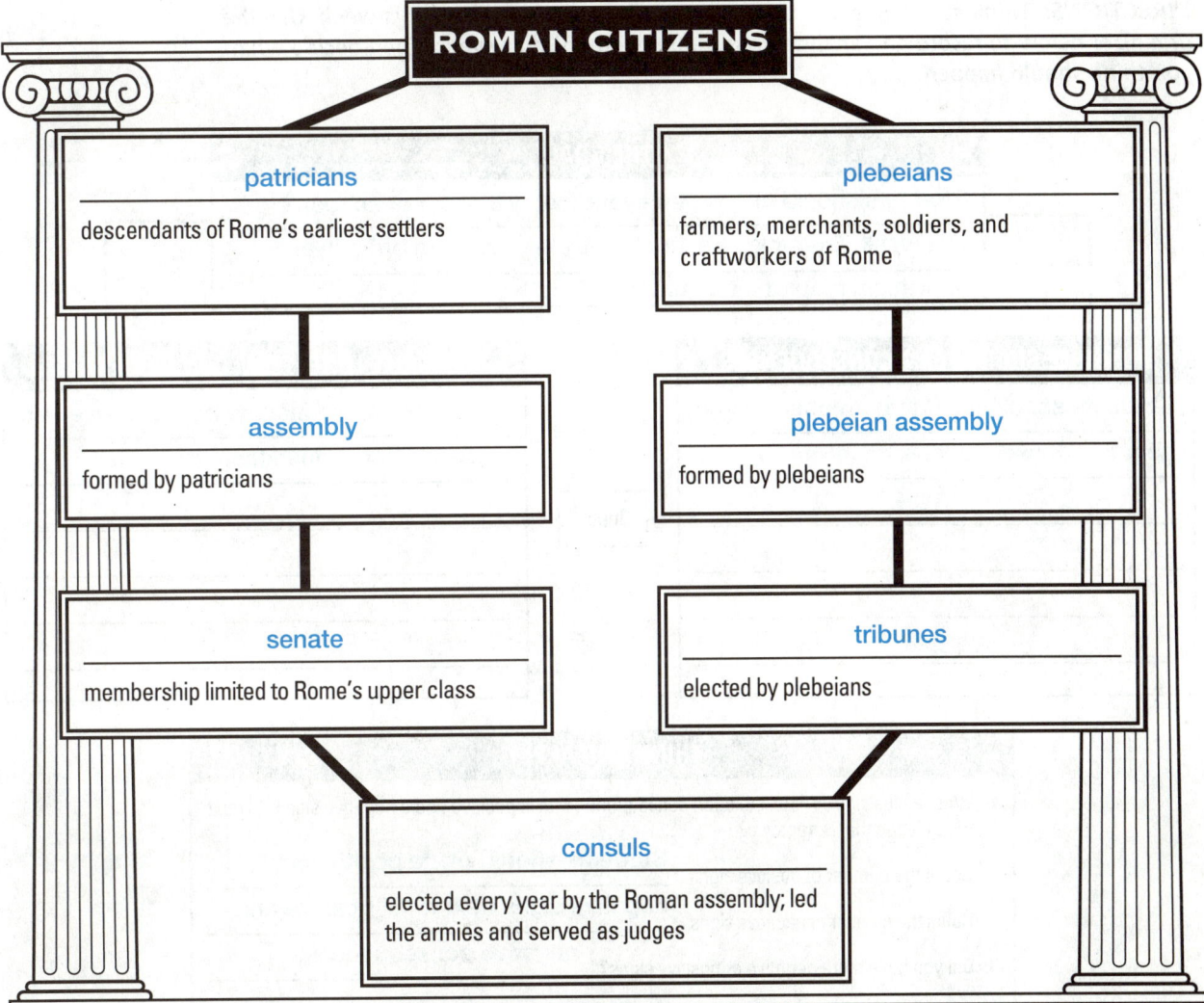

ROMAN CITIZENS

- **patricians** — descendants of Rome's earliest settlers
- **plebeians** — farmers, merchants, soldiers, and craftworkers of Rome
- **assembly** — formed by patricians
- **plebeian assembly** — formed by plebeians
- **senate** — membership limited to Rome's upper class
- **tribunes** — elected by plebeians
- **consuls** — elected every year by the Roman assembly; led the armies and served as judges

1. How many consuls were elected each year? **2**
2. What were the plebeians' special officials called? **tribunes**
3. How did the tribunes exercise power? **veto**
4. What special action could Romans take in an emergency? **appoint a dictator**

Use after reading Chapter 8, Lesson 2, pages 331–337.

NAME _____ DATE _____

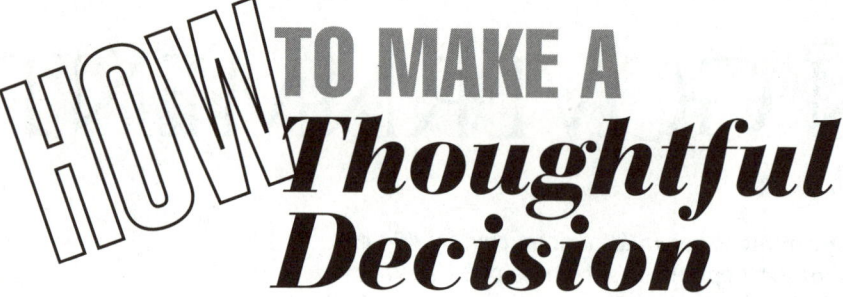

HOW TO MAKE A Thoughtful Decision

Apply Critical Thinking Skills

DIRECTIONS: Think about an event that will take place at your school this week. Use the organizer below to record and analyze your thoughts about that event. Then decide what you think should happen.

THE GOAL
Students should choose an event that will occur at school this week. Example: A school club plans to hand out a flyer showing a map of the countries of the world.

POSSIBLE SHORT-TERM CONSEQUENCES
Students should include both positive and negative consequences.

POSSIBLE LONG-TERM CONSEQUENCES
Students should include both positive and negative consequences.

Input

THINK AND APPLY
1. Write a plus sign (+) next to each consequence that is positive and a negative sign (−) next to each one that is negative.
2. Count the number of positive signs. ___ Students should place positive and
   Count the number of negative signs. ___ negative signs next to all positive and
3. Did you have more negative or positive signs? ___ negative consequences.

YOU DECIDE
Given the positive and negative consequences of this event, do you think it should take place as scheduled? Or, do you think you should suggest making changes in the event based on the consequences?
Students' answers will vary.

NAME _____ DATE _____

THE ROMAN EMPIRE

Break Information into Small Pieces

DIRECTIONS: *It is easier to learn material when it is in small pieces. This lesson has four sections, each of which is listed below. Use your textbook to answer the questions under each section.*

Rome Becomes an Empire

1. What event left Rome without a leader? **the death of Julius Caesar**

2. What significant event happened in 31 B.C.? **Octavian defeated Antony and Cleopatra and gained leadership of all Roman lands.**

3. Who was Rome's first true emperor? **Octavian (Augustus)**

The Age of Augustus

1. What was the *Pax Romana*? **a time of peace and unity for Rome**

2. Give an example of a law passed by the Romans. **People cannot be forced to speak against themselves in a court of law.**

3. What was the purpose of the first Roman census? **to let the government know how many people were in the empire, so that all could be taxed**

4. What was the main purpose of the Roman road system? **to allow quick movement of Roman legions from province to province**

Pride in Rome

1. What is a basilica? **a huge marble building often used for government**

2. What was the name of Rome's largest arena? **the Colosseum**

3. What is an aqueduct? **a combination of bridges and canals that carry water from place to place**

Arts, Literature, and Language

1. What is meant by the phrase, "Conquered Greece conquered its uncultured conqueror and brought the arts to Rome"? **The Romans, who had conquered Greece, copied Greek culture. They borrowed Greek ideas for architecture, art, writing style, and philosophy.**

2. What language became common throughout the Roman Empire? **Latin**

Use after reading Chapter 8, Lesson 3, pages 340–347.

NAME _____ DATE _____

How to Compare Historical Maps

Apply Map and Globe Skills

DIRECTIONS: Use the two maps on this page to answer the questions that follow.

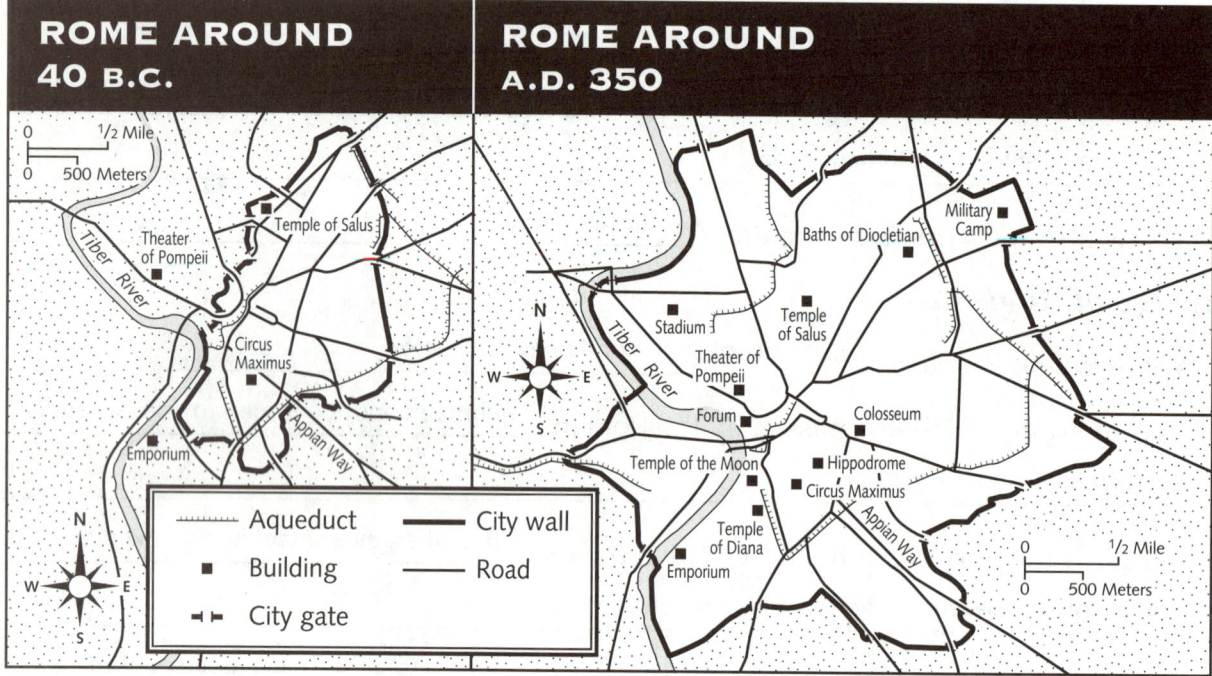

1. How many years' difference is there between these two maps? **390 years**

2. What physical feature is common to both maps? **the Tiber River**

3. In 40 B.C. was the Theater of Pompeii inside or outside the city wall? **outside**

4. In A.D. 350 was the stadium inside or outside the city wall? **inside**

5. In 40 B.C. how many openings were there in the wall? **15**

    in A.D. 350? **18**

6. What formed most of the western boundary of Rome in A.D. 350? **the Tiber River**

NAME _____ DATE _____

ROMAN MILITARY MIGHT

Apply Information

DIRECTIONS: Read the paragraph and study the diagram. Then complete the activity.

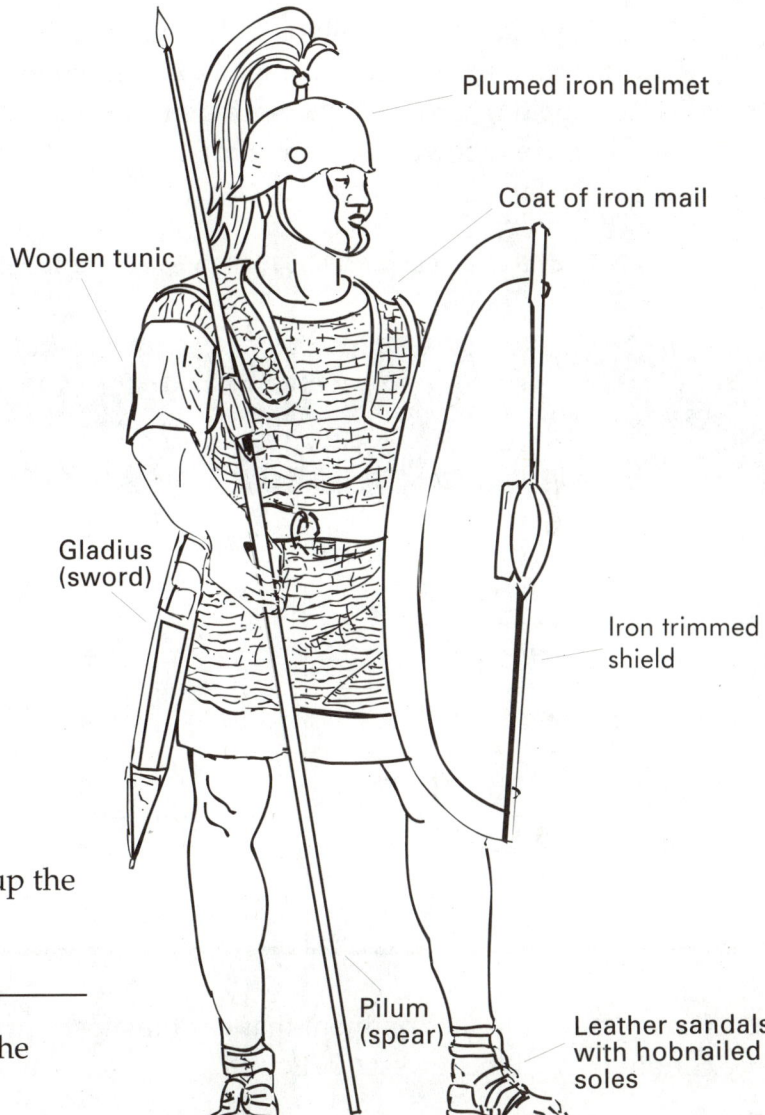

The power of Caesar's Rome rested in its military machine. The Roman army was made up of 28 legions, each commanded by a general. Each legion was composed of 10 cohorts with about 500 men, including officers and 480 legionaries, or footsoldiers. Cohorts were divided into 6 centuries of 80 men each, and each century was further divided into squads of 8 soldiers, called contubernia.

1. How many legionaries made up the Roman army?
   134,400 (480 × 10 × 28)

2. What protective clothing did the legionaries wear?
   coat of iron mail, iron helmet with ear flaps, shield

3. What weapons did the Roman soldier carry?
   sword and spear

4. On a separate sheet of paper, make an organizational chart of a Roman legion.

Use after reading Chapter 8, Lesson 4, pages 350–353.

ACTIVITY BOOK 77

NAME _____ DATE _____

Christianity Today

Christianity has nearly 2 billion followers worldwide, more than any other religion. Christians worship in various ways. Christian churches, and the denominations to which they belong, are organized differently. However, all Christians, whatever their denomination, are followers of Jesus Christ.

Compare Populations

DIRECTIONS: Study the comparison table. Then complete the activities that follow.

CHRISTIAN POPULATION BY CONTINENT, 1995 (in millions)							
	TOTAL POPULATION	TOTAL CHRISTIANS	ROMAN CATHOLIC	PROTESTANTS	ORTHODOX	ANGLICAN (CHURCH OF ENGLAND)	OTHERS
Africa	728.0	348.2	122.1	109.7	29.6	25.4	61.3
Asia	3,458.0	306.8	90.0	42.8	14.9	0.7	158.3
Europe **M**	727.0	551.9	270.7	80.0	165.8	30.6	4.8
(South America)	482.0	448.0	402.7	31.7	0.5	1.2	12.0
North America	292.8	249.3	74.2	123.2	6.5	6.8	38.5
Australia **L**	28.5	23.8	8.3	8.4	0.7	5.9	0.7
World	5,716.4	1,928.0	968.0	395.8	218.0	70.5	275.6

1. Put an *M* next to the continent that has the most Christians. Put an *L* next to the continent with the fewest Christians.

2. Compare the number of Christians in Europe with the total European population. Are Christians in the majority or minority? __majority__

3. On which continent or continents are there more Protestants than Roman Catholics?
North America, Australia

4. Which continent has the highest percentage of Christians? Circle it.

5. What percentage of the world population is Christian? __33.7%__

HOW TO READ A Telescoping Time Line

Chart and Graph Skills

DIRECTIONS: The time line below shows some of the key dates in the history of ancient Greece and the Roman Empire. One section of the time line has been expanded to show some dates that could not have been shown at the scale of the main time line. Use these two time lines to complete the questions on page 80.

TELESCOPING TIME LINE

Main time line:
- 776 B.C. — Greeks hold first Olympic Games
- 753 B.C. — Rome founded
- 500 B.C. — Rome establishes a republic
- 432 B.C. — Construction of Parthenon completed
- 146 B.C. — End of last Punic War
- 44 B.C. — Assassination of Julius Caesar
- 27 B.C. — Beginning of the Roman Empire
- A.D. 79 — Pompeii destroyed
- A.D. 80 — Construction of Colosseum completed

Scale markers: 800 B.C., 700 B.C., 600 B.C., 500 B.C., 400 B.C., 300 B.C., 200 B.C., 100 B.C., 0, A.D. 100, A.D. 200

Expanded section (340 B.C. – 320 B.C.):
- Alexander becomes king of Macedonia
- 335 B.C. — Alexander defeats Persians at Tyre and Gaza
- 330 B.C. — Alexander defeats Persians at Gaugamela
- Alexander defeats Persians at Persepolis and Bactra-Zauspa
- 325 B.C. — Death of Alexander the Great

(Continued)

Use after reading Chapter 8, Skill Lesson, page 361.

NAME _____ DATE _____

1. When was Rome founded? 753 B.C.

2. In what year did Alexander defeat the Persians at Bactra-Zauspa?
   330 B.C.

3. What event in Roman history took place 17 years after the assassination of Julius Caesar?
   beginning of the Roman Empire

4. Which was completed first, the Colosseum or the Parthenon?
   the Parthenon

5. How long after Alexander became king of Macedonia did he die?
   13 years

6. When did the last Punic War end? 146 B.C.

7. Which part of the time line has been expanded with a larger scale?
   the part dealing with the military campaign of Alexander the Great in the Persian Empire; the part from 340 B.C. to 320 B.C.

8. Why is the telescoping time line helpful? Without it, the information showing Alexander's military campaigns would have to be condensed into too small a space.

The GERMANIC TRIBES

Apply Information

DIRECTIONS: Read the definitions. Then use your textbook to fill in the puzzle with the correct answers.

```
        1 V  I  S  I  G  O  T  H  2 S
          A                       A
      3 F R  A  N  K  S           X
          D                       O
          A              4 H  U  N  S
          L                       S
          S
```

Across

1. Led by Alaric, they captured Rome in A.D. 410 and looted the city.

3. With the leader Clovis, they captured the last Roman territory in Gaul in A.D. 486.

4. People from central Asia who took over Germanic lands.

Down

1. Attacked Rome in A.D. 455 and stole items of value.

2. With the Angles they captured Britain.

Use after reading Chapter 8, Lesson 6, pages 362–365.

NAME _____ DATE _____

Ancient Rome

Connect Main Ideas

DIRECTIONS: Use this organizer to show the growth of the Roman Empire and the changes it faced. Write two details to support each main idea.

Geography of Ancient Rome
The geography of the Italian peninsula contributed to the rise of ancient Roman civilization.

1. Students should mention that travel and trade by land in Italy was easier than by sea because Italy has few good harbors.
2. The people of Italy traded more with each other than with people across the seas.

The Roman Republic
Over the years the government of Rome changed.

1. Students should mention that Rome's government went from a monarchy to a republic to a
2. dictatorship.

Ancient Rome

The Roman Empire
Many peoples were united under the Roman Empire.

1. Students may mention Augustus as Rome's first emperor and that during his rule peace,
2. pride in Rome, arts, and language helped unite the empire.

Beginnings of Christianity
Christianity spread throughout the Roman Empire.

1. Students may mention the beginning of Christianity, the ways Christianity grew, the people who helped
2. bring growth to Christianity, and the acceptance of Christianity in the empire.

Rome's Decline in the West
Roman rule weakened in the western half of the Roman Empire.

1. Students may mention the ending of the *Pax Romana,* the split of the empire, and the
2. invasion of the Germanic tribes.

82 ACTIVITY BOOK   Use after reading Chapter 8, pages 326–367.

NAME _____ DATE _____

FINDING PLACES in South America

Locate Places on a Map

DIRECTIONS: Study the map on page 84. Then answer the questions and complete the activities below.

1. Name the latitude that is closest to the city of Quito.
   Equator, 0°

2. Circle the name of the largest country in South America. What is its name?
   Brazil

3. A city at 30°S, 50°W is
   Porto Alegre

4. Between which labeled meridians does Buenos Aires lie?
   between 50°W and 60°W

5. When goods are transported from Asunción to ports on the Atlantic Ocean, in what direction would they go and which borders would they cross?
   most likely south, across the border of Argentina, and east to the ocean; or east or northeast
   across Paraguay, across the border of Brazil, and east to the ocean

6. The Amazon is the longest river in South America. Label it and trace it in blue.

7. The Falkland Islands belong to the United Kingdom (Great Britain). How far are they from Argentina? about 400 miles (644 km)

8. Venezuela, Chile, Ecuador, Guyana, and Uruguay are not labeled. Add their labels to the map. You may want to use an atlas to help you.

(Continued)

NAME _____ DATE _____

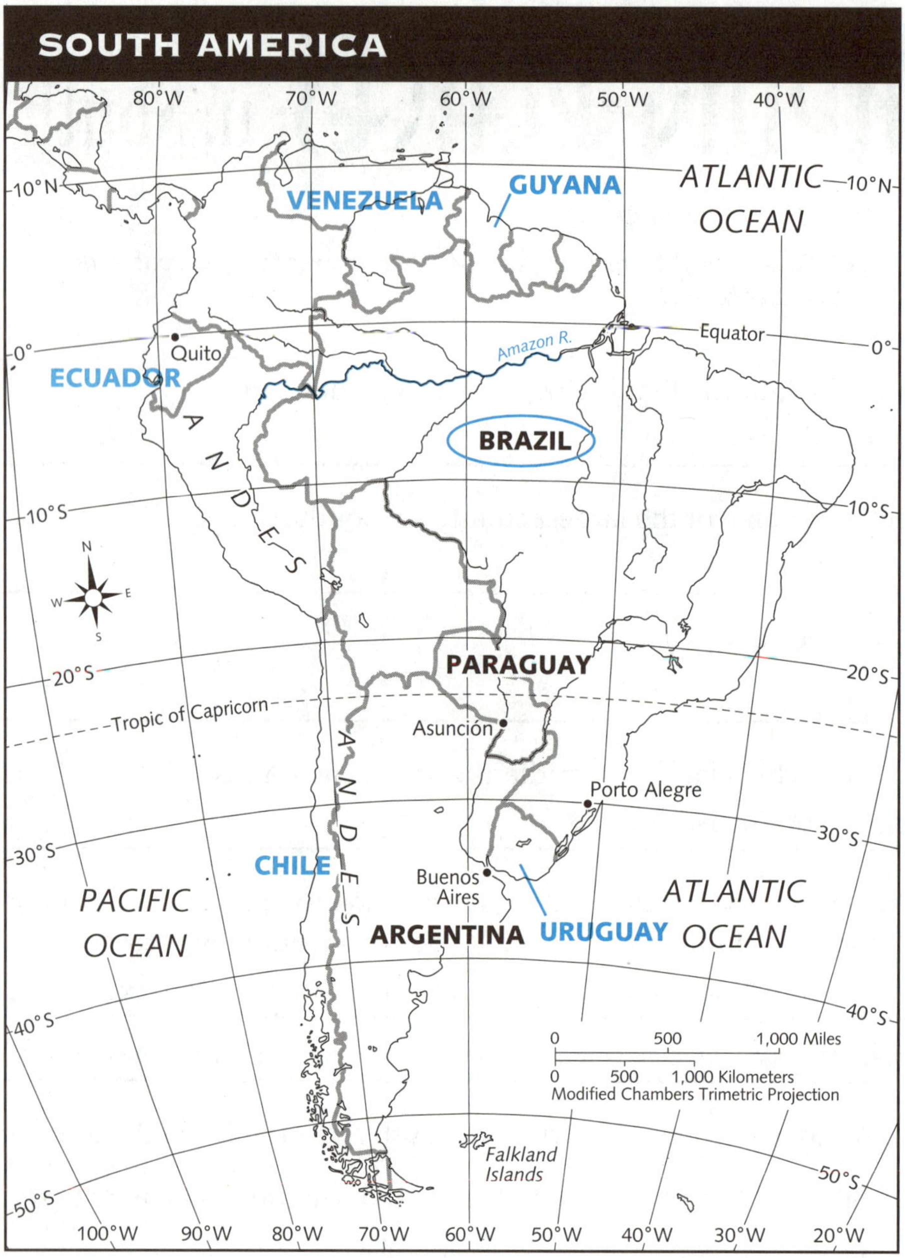

SOUTH AMERICA

84 ACTIVITY BOOK Use after reading Chapter 9, Lesson 1, pages 383–387.

NAME _____ DATE _____

Olmec ACCOMPLISHMENTS

Compare Cultures

DIRECTIONS: Examine the list of accomplishments of the Olmecs. Then complete the activities that follow.

A. __R__ Gigantic heads

B. __T__ Farm crops

C. __R__ Ritual ball game

D. __R, S__ Hieroglyphics

E. __R__ Small sculptured objects

F. __R__ Temples on platforms

G. __T__ Rubber

H. __S__ The tumpline

I. __S__ Recorded amounts in trade transactions

J. __S__ Recorded when to plant and when to harvest

1. Label with an *R* those Olmec accomplishments that might have influenced the religion of other people in Mesoamerica.

2. Label with an *S* those items that might have been used in mathematics, science, and technology.

3. Label with the letter *T* those items that the Olmecs might have traded with other peoples.

4. Which achievement might have led to the development of a calendar? __J__

5. What is intercropping and how did it help the Olmec economy?
   Intercropping — the planting together of beans, squash, and corn; it increased the crop yield and gave the Olmecs harvested foods ample enough to trade with others.

6. Why are the Olmecs sometimes called the "mother civilization" of Mesoamerica?
   so much of the religion, technology, and language of the Olmecs influenced other civilizations that came later in Mesoamerica

Use after reading Chapter 9, Lesson 2, pages 388–393.

NAME _____ DATE _____

HOW TO LEARN FROM ARTIFACTS

Apply Critical Thinking Skills

DIRECTIONS: Below are drawings of artifacts from three different civilizations and three different parts of the world. Study the drawings and read the descriptions. Draw a line from each drawing to the description that correctly identifies it. Then answer the questions that follow.

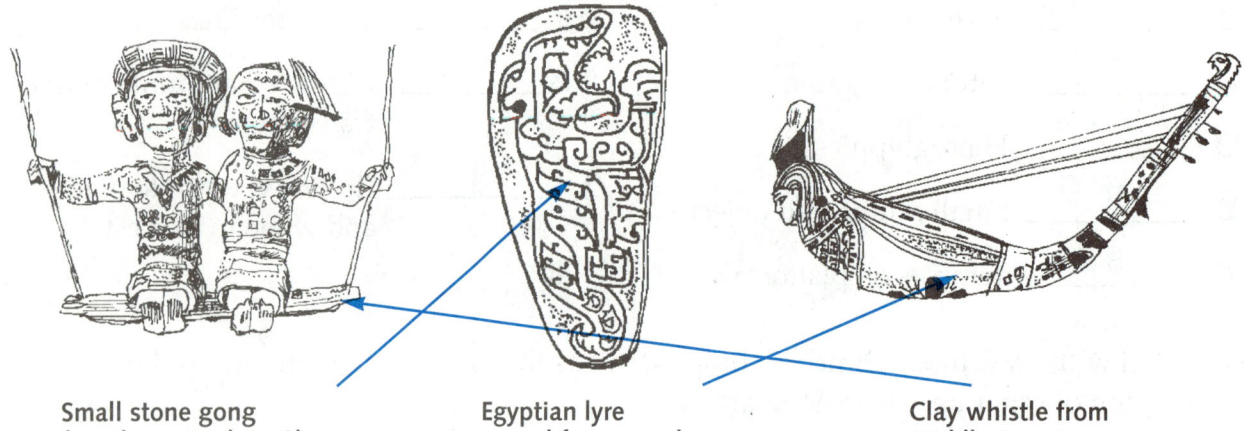

Small stone gong found in a tomb in China

Egyptian lyre carved from wood

Clay whistle from Middle America

1. What is the common purpose of the three artifacts shown above?
They are all musical instruments.

2. What do these artifacts tell you about the people who made them?
They had the time and ability to create music and art.

Use after reading Chapter 9, Skill Lesson, pages 394–395.

MAYAN *Math*

The ancient Mayas used just three different symbols to make all their numbers. Shells (🐚) stood for zero, dots (•) for ones, and bars (—) for fives. The Mayan numbers 0 to 19 are shown below.

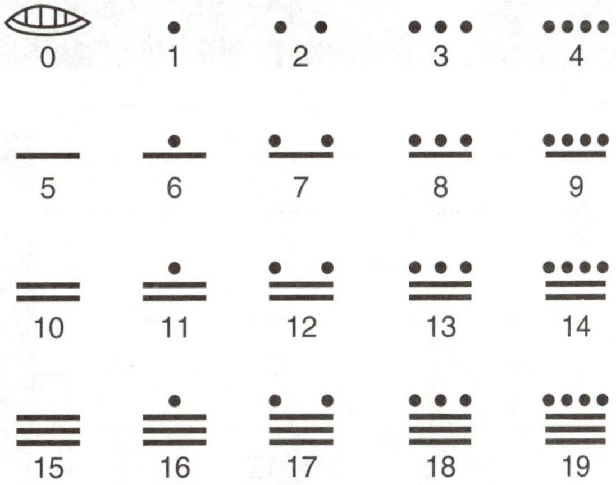

0	1	2	3	4
5	6	7	8	9
10	11	12	13	14
15	16	17	18	19

Apply Knowledge to a New Situation

DIRECTIONS: The mathematics problems below have Mayan numbers instead of the numbers you use. For each problem, fill in the missing Mayan numbers.

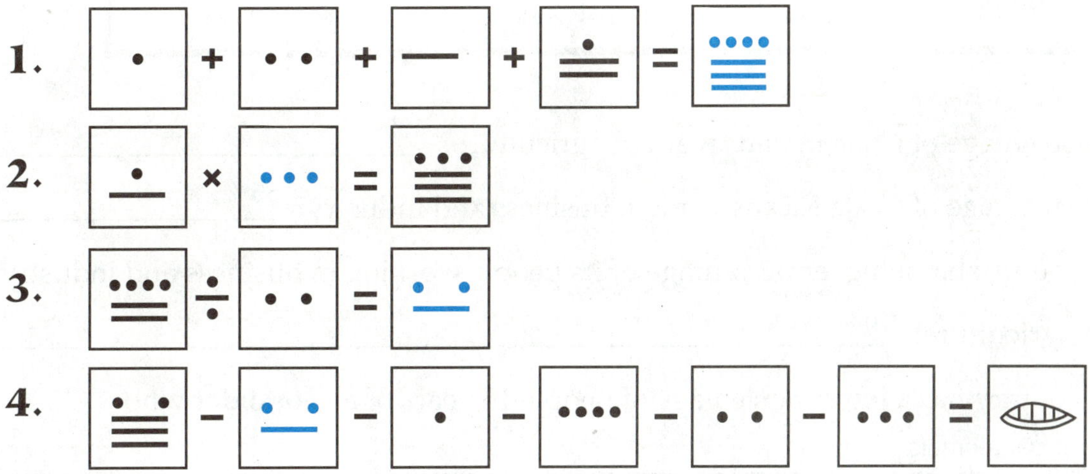

1. 1 + 2 + 5 + 6 = 14
2. 6 × 3 = 18
3. 14 ÷ 2 = 7
4. 12 − 7 − 1 − 4 − 2 − 3 = 0

Use after reading Chapter 9, Lesson 3, pages 396–401.

ACTIVITY BOOK 87

NAME _____ DATE _____

HOW TO USE A Double-Bar Graph

Apply Chart and Graph Skills

DIRECTIONS: Study the double-bar graph comparing some facts about the people of Costa Rica and the people of Guatemala. Then answer the questions that follow.

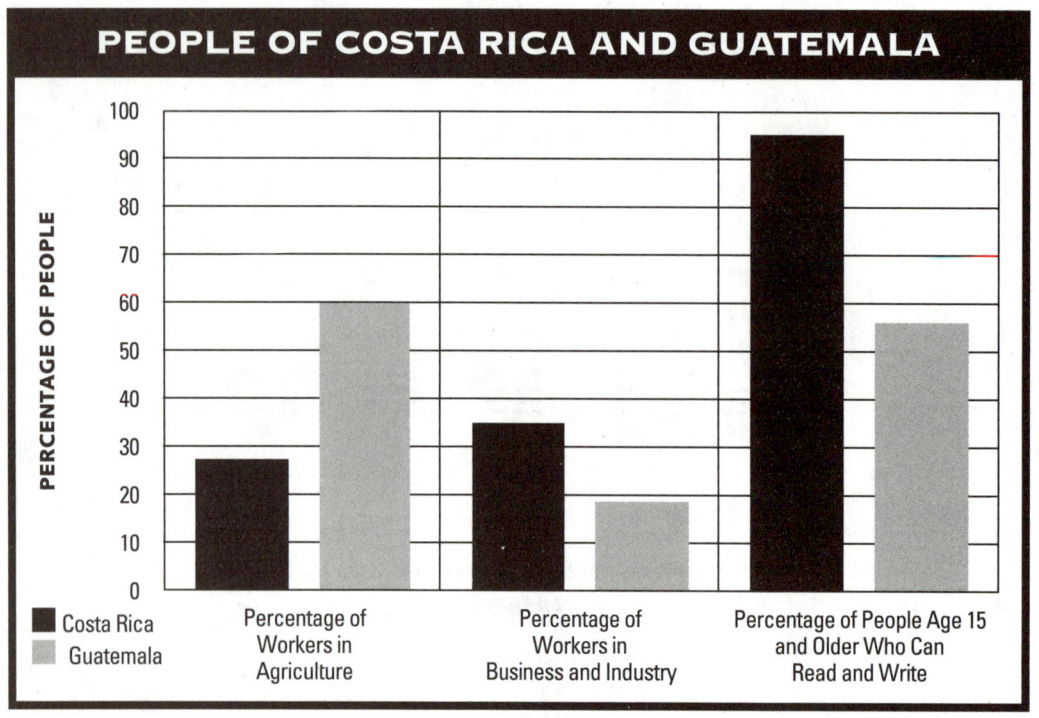

1. What percentage of Guatemalans work in agriculture? __60%__

2. What percentage of Costa Ricans work in business and industry? __35%__

3. Which country has a higher percentage of its people working in business and industry than in agriculture? __Costa Rica__

4. Which country has a lower percentage of people 15 years of age or older who can read? __Guatemala__

5. Why do you think there are many differences between Costa Rica and Guatemala? __Guatemala's economy is more farm based; Costa Rica, with a much higher literacy rate, might encourage people to enter nonfarming jobs, such as those in business and industry.__

88 ACTIVITY BOOK   Use after reading Chapter 9, Skill Lesson, pages 402–403.

NAME _____ DATE _____

The OLMECS and the MAYAS

Connect Main Ideas

DIRECTIONS: Use this organizer to tell about early civilizations in the Americas. Write two examples for each main idea.

Geography of the Americas
Early people migrated from Asia to North America across a land bridge.

1. Students should mention that the geography of the Americas affected where the early people hunted, gathered, and eventually settled.
2.

The Olmecs
The Olmecs created a civilization that affected the development of other civilizations in Mesoamerica.

1. Students may mention that the Olmecs are considered the "Mother Civilization" and that later civilizations in Mesoamerica
2. adopted Olmec language, religion, and technology.

The Olmecs and the Mayas

The Mayas
The long-lasting Mayan civilization is remembered for its many achievements.

1. Students may mention that the Mayas were skilled architects and builders; that they developed a
2. system of writing and a calendar.

Use after reading Chapter 9, pages 382–405.

ACTIVITY BOOK 89

NAME _____   DATE _____

THE Aztecs

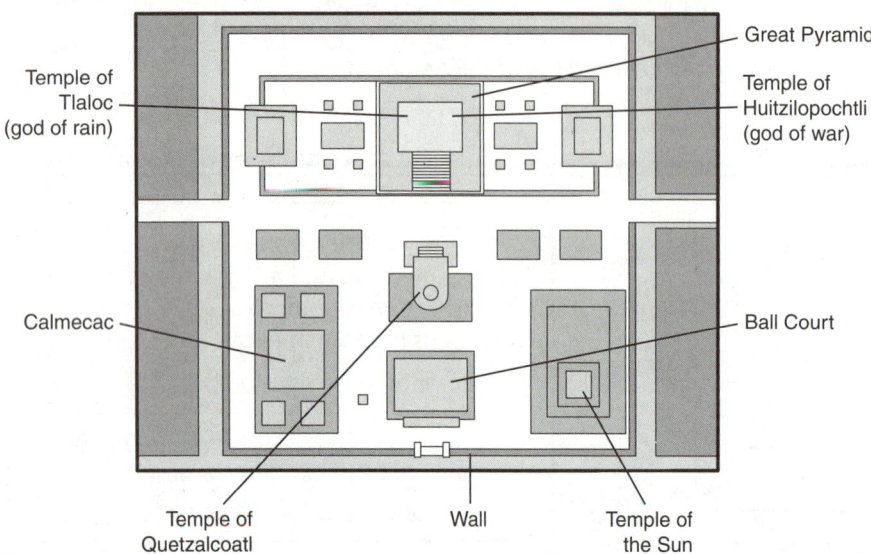

Within the city of Tenochtitlán was the religious center of the Aztec people. The religious center, an area surrounded by walls, consisted of several temples honoring different Aztec gods. The site included a ball court and a *calmecac*, or a school to train Aztec children for religious, military, or political life.

Interpret a Diagram

DIRECTIONS: Look at the diagram of Tenochtitlán. Then answer the questions.

1. Why do you think there were many temples in Tenochtitlán?
The Aztecs had many gods, and each temple was for a different one.

2. At the top of the Great Pyramid were twin temples to the Aztec gods of rain and war. Why do you think the pyramid was designed this way?
The gods of rain and war must have been of great and equal importance to the Aztecs.

3. Why do you think a ball court was on the temple grounds?
The ball game had a religious meaning.

4. The Aztecs' economy was based on agriculture. How is this shown in the temples of Tenochtitlán? Among the temples were those dedicated to the gods of rain and sun, both very important to agriculture; at the temples the Aztecs must have prayed to the gods of rain and sun for favorable weather conditions for a good harvest.

NAME _____ DATE _____

HOW TO COMPARE Maps with Different Scales

Apply Map and Globe Skills

DIRECTIONS: Look at the main map of Mexico and the inset map of Mexico and its neighbors. Then answer the questions below in the space provided.

____main map____ 1. Which map is better for measuring the distance between Guatemala and Monterrey?

____inset map____ 2. Which map is better for measuring the distance between Honduras and the United States border?

____main map____ 3. Find Veracruz, a city that is located near some of Mexico's oldest archaeological sites. Which map did you use to find it?

____$2\frac{1}{2}$ inches____ 4. About how many inches are used to show 1,000 miles on the main map?

____$\frac{1}{2}$ inch____ 5. What is the approximate measurement of 1,000 miles on the inset map?

____650 miles____ 6. About how many miles is it between La Paz and Mexicali?

Use after reading Chapter 10, Skill Lesson, pages 412–413.

NAME _____ DATE _____

To Market, To Market Aztec Style

Compare Cultures

DIRECTIONS: When the Spanish conquistadors arrived in the Aztec Empire looking for gold, they were impressed by the great market at Tlatelolco (tlah·tay·LOL·koh). However, the Aztecs and conquistadors had different ideas of what items at the market were most valuable. Below is a list of items that might have been found at the Aztec market. In the column labeled Aztecs, number the goods from 1 to 12, with 1 being the item you think was the most valuable to the Aztecs and 12 being the item of least value. Do the same for the column labeled Conquistadors. This time, number the items according to which ones you think were most valuable to the Spanish conquistadors.

	Aztecs	Conquistadors
Mantles or cloaks	Accept all	
Cacao beans	reasonable	
Fruits, vegetables, meat, fish	student	
Slaves	responses.	
Pottery and baskets		
Bright-colored parrot feathers		
Animal skins		
Copper axes		
Jade, imported turquoise, silver, and gold		
Goose quills full of gold dust		
Maize of many kinds and colors		
Sandals made of cactus fiber, cotton capes and skirts		

92 ACTIVITY BOOK   Use after reading Chapter 10, Lesson 2, pages 414–417.

NAME _____   DATE _____

INCA Record Keeping

Study Cultures Through Artifacts

DIRECTIONS: Read the following paragraph, and study the drawing on the right. Then answer the questions that follow.

The Incas had no written language or numbers. Instead, they recorded important information on string devices known as quipus (KEE•pooz). The colors and twists of the grouped strings designated what was being counted. The knots showed the totals. The Incas based their method of counting on a decimal system like ours. The number *0* was indicated by the lack of a knot. This system of keeping records required a special class in Inca society of trained quipu interpreters.

1. What kinds of things do you think would have to be counted in a society such as the Incas had? Responses may include population, tax payments, food production, storage, and distribution.

2. Why do you think people would have to be specially trained to read and keep records using quipus? It was a complicated system that would take a long time to learn and a lot of practice to remember.

3. What quality of the Incas do you think use of the quipu indicates?
They had to be highly organized, logical thinkers.

4. To communicate with the people, the Inca ruler sent out messengers. How do you suppose the runners carried the ruler's decrees and orders? Without a written language, they would have had to memorize his decrees and pass them along to other runners who did the same.

Use after reading Chapter 10, Lesson 3, pages 418–423.

NAME _____   DATE _____

HOW TO EVALUATE Information and Sources

Apply Reading and Research Skills

DIRECTIONS: Read each of the following situations. Answer the question at the end of each situation.

1. You are an archaeologist. You have just returned from a dig in Mexico, where you found an ancient codex. The codex tells about the founding of an ancient Aztec city. The people living in the city today tell a completely different story of the city's founding. Which story do you believe? Explain.

Student responses may vary. Some may say that they believe the ancient writing because it is a primary source. Others may argue that it may be exaggerated or not a truthful account. They may say that the people living today probably had the true story passed down to them through the many generations that came before them.

2. You are researching information about the ancient Incas for a school report. Your library has 30 books about the Incas. What questions might you ask yourself to decide which books you will choose?

Questions students might ask include the following: What is the date of publication for each book? What qualifications does each author have to write about the Incas? Which book discusses more fully the topic to be included in the research report? Which book uses primary sources? Which book is easiest for students to understand? Which books do other people recommend?

Use after reading Chapter 10, Skill Lesson, pages 424–425.

NAME _____ DATE _____

The Aztecs and the Incas

Connect Main Ideas

DIRECTIONS: Use this organizer to show how the Aztecs and the Incas built their empires. Write two examples for each main idea.

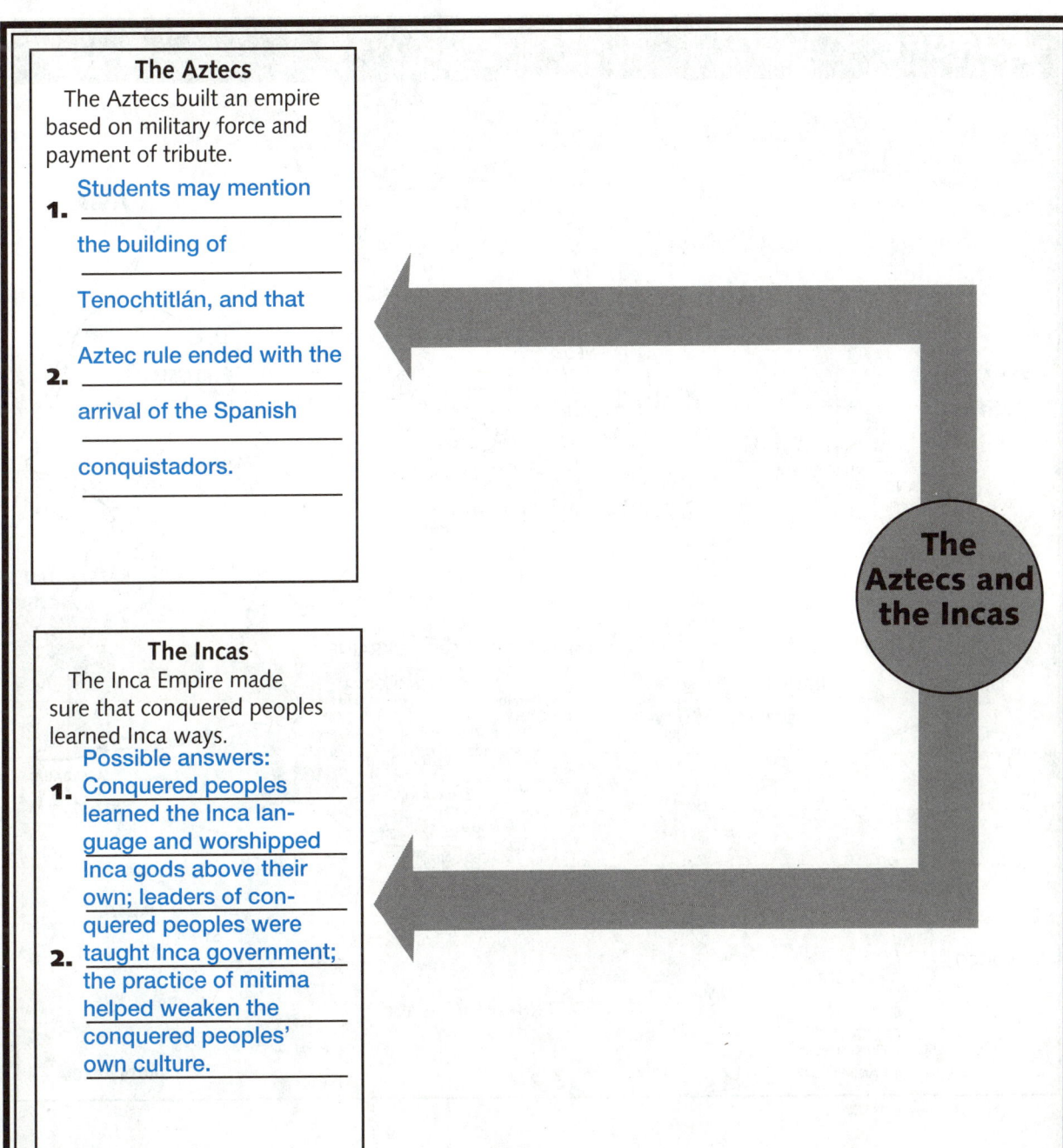

The Aztecs
The Aztecs built an empire based on military force and payment of tribute.

1. Students may mention the building of Tenochtitlán, and that

2. Aztec rule ended with the arrival of the Spanish conquistadors.

The Incas
The Inca Empire made sure that conquered peoples learned Inca ways.

Possible answers:
1. Conquered peoples learned the Inca language and worshipped Inca gods above their own; leaders of conquered peoples were
2. taught Inca government; the practice of mitima helped weaken the conquered peoples' own culture.

The Aztecs and the Incas

Use after reading Chapter 10, pages 406–427.

NAME _____ DATE _____

Europe Today

Locate Places on a Map

DIRECTIONS: Look at the map of Europe below. Then answer the questions on the next page.

(Continued)

96 ACTIVITY BOOK   Use after reading Chapter 11, Lesson 1, pages 445–451.

NAME _____ DATE _____

1. Which country occupies the largest land area in Europe?
   Russia

2. Which country has Minsk as its capital?
   Belarus

3. Which European country is farthest west? What is its approximate location?
   Iceland; 65°N, 20°W

4. Which countries are in both Europe and Asia?
   Russia, Turkey, Kazakhstan, Azerbaijan, Georgia

5. In what important way are Spain, France, and Italy similar in terms of geography?
   They are on the Mediterranean Sea.

6. Which countries border the Czech Republic? What direction is each from the Czech Republic?
   Germany is to the west and northwest, Austria is to the south, Slovakia is to the southeast, and Poland is to the northeast.

7. Which countries have parts that are within the Arctic Circle?
   Iceland, Norway, Sweden, Finland, Russia

8. In which direction would you fly to travel directly from Norway to Turkey?
   southeast

9. What separates the United Kingdom (Great Britain) from the rest of Europe?
   the English Channel and the North Sea

Use after reading Chapter 11, Lesson 1, pages 445–451.

NAME _____ DATE _____

HOW TO COMPARE Population Maps

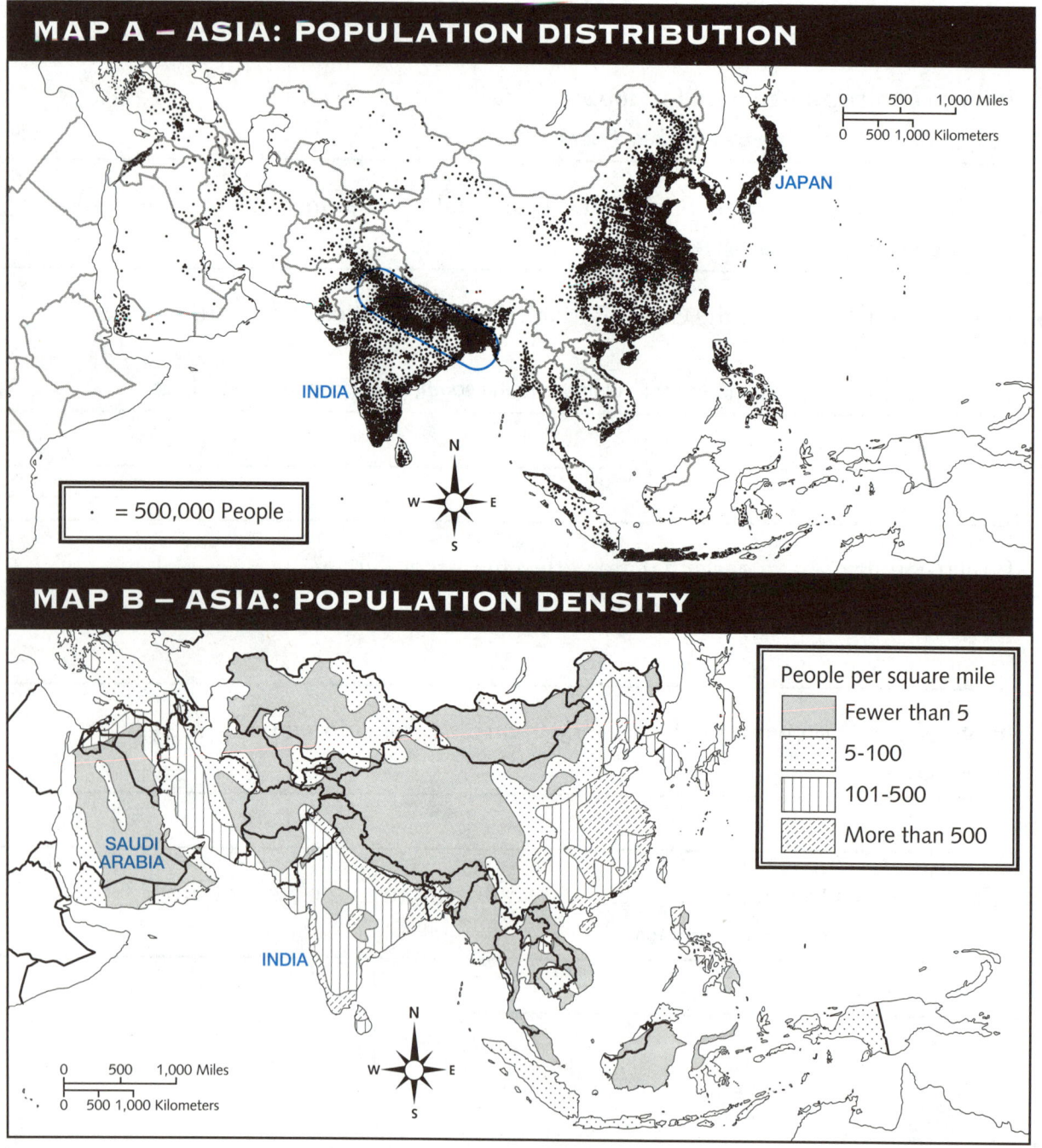

(Continued)

98 ACTIVITY BOOK   Use after reading Chapter 11, Skill Lesson, pages 452–453.

NAME _____ DATE _____

Apply Map and Globe Skills

DIRECTIONS: Study the two maps on page 98. Both show population density. Map A shows density using dots. Map B uses different patterns to show different levels of population density. Use these two maps to complete the activities below.

1. Label Japan on Map A. How would you describe the distribution of dots in Japan?
   There are so many of them that most of the country is solid black.

2. Find Japan on Map B. What is the population density for most of the country?
   101–500 people per square mile

3. Which area of Asia is most densely populated? least densely populated? Explain your answers. Most: coastlines; least: interior; Accept answers that refer to the climate, access to water, and historical development of the country.

4. Label Saudi Arabia on Map B. What is the population density of most of Saudi Arabia?
   fewer than 5 people per square mile

5. On Map A, label India. Circle the heavy concentration of dots in northern India. What does this heavy concentration of dots tell you about the population of the area?
   that it is very densely populated

6. Find and label India on Map B. What is the population density of the area you circled on Map A? more than 500 people per square mile

7. What conclusions might you be able to draw about this part of the world based on its population? Possible responses may include that most people live near the coast where there is mild weather and there is access to transportation.

8. Which map provides the best overall view of where the heaviest population areas are in Asia? Explain your answer. Map A, because the high density of dots makes some areas look black, allowing the viewer to make the connection that a large number of dots equals dense populations.

9. Which map would you use if you wanted to know the specific number of people living in a part of China? Explain your answer.
   Map B, because it provides information on the number of people per square mile.

Use after reading Chapter 11, Skill Lesson, pages 452–453.

NAME _____ DATE _____

Recent Immigrants to the United States

Read a Table for Information

DIRECTIONS: Study the tables below. Then answer the questions on the next page.

IMMIGRATION FOR YEAR 1996
TOP 10 COUNTRIES OF BIRTH

COUNTRY OF BIRTH	TO UNITED STATES
Mexico	163,572
Philippines	55,876
India	44,859
Vietnam	42,067
China	41,728
Dominican Republic	39,604
Cuba	26,466
Ukraine	21,079
Russia	19,668
Jamaica	19,089
All countries	915,900

Table A

IMMIGRATION FOR YEARS 1981–1996
TOP 10 COUNTRIES OF BIRTH

COUNTRY OF BIRTH	TO UNITED STATES
Mexico	3,304,682
Philippines	843,741
Vietnam	719,239
China	539,267
Dominican Republic	509,902
India	498,309
Korea	453,018
El Salvador	362,225
Jamaica	323,625
Cuba	254,193
All countries	13,484,275

Table B

IMMIGRANTS, PLANNED RESIDENCE, 1996
TOP 10 METROPOLITAN AREAS

METROPOLITAN AREA	IMMIGRANTS
New York, NY	133,168
Los Angeles–Long Beach, CA	64,285
Miami, FL	41,527
Chicago, IL	39,989
Washington, DC, MD, VA	34,327
Houston, TX	21,387
Boston, Lawrence, Lowell, Brockton, MA	18,726
San Diego, CA	18,226
San Francisco, CA	18,171
Newark, NJ	17,939
All Areas	915,900

Table C

(continued)

100 ACTIVITY BOOK

Use after reading Chapter 11, Lesson 2, pages 454–461.

NAME _____ DATE _____

1. From which country have the most immigrants arrived since 1981?

   Mexico

2. From which continent did most immigrants come in 1996?

   Asia

3. Of the ten countries on Table A, which do not appear on Table B?

   Ukraine and Russia

4. Why do you think there are countries on the top 10 list for 1996 that were not on the top 10 list for the years 1981–1996?

   Perhaps political or economic conditions have changed in those countries; perhaps it is easier for people to leave these countries; perhaps conditions are worse, and people want to start over in a new country.

5. To which state did most of the immigrants plan to move in 1996?

   New York

6. Did more immigrants plan to live in Miami or in San Diego?

   Miami

7. Did most immigrants in 1996 plan to move to the top metropolitan areas? Explain your answer. No; the total of immigrants for the top 10 metropolitan areas is a little less than half the total immigrants moving to all areas.

8. According to Table C, what percentage of immigrants planned to live in California? Show how you reached your answer.

   11 percent; the total immigrants planning to move to the three California metropolitan areas was 100,682, or about 11 percent of 915,900, the total of all immigrants.

Use after reading Chapter 11, Lesson 2, pages 454–461.

ACTIVITY BOOK 101

NAME _____ DATE _____

HOW TO UNDERSTAND A TIME ZONE MAP

Apply Map and Globe Skills

DIRECTIONS: Study the map below. Then complete the activities on the next page.

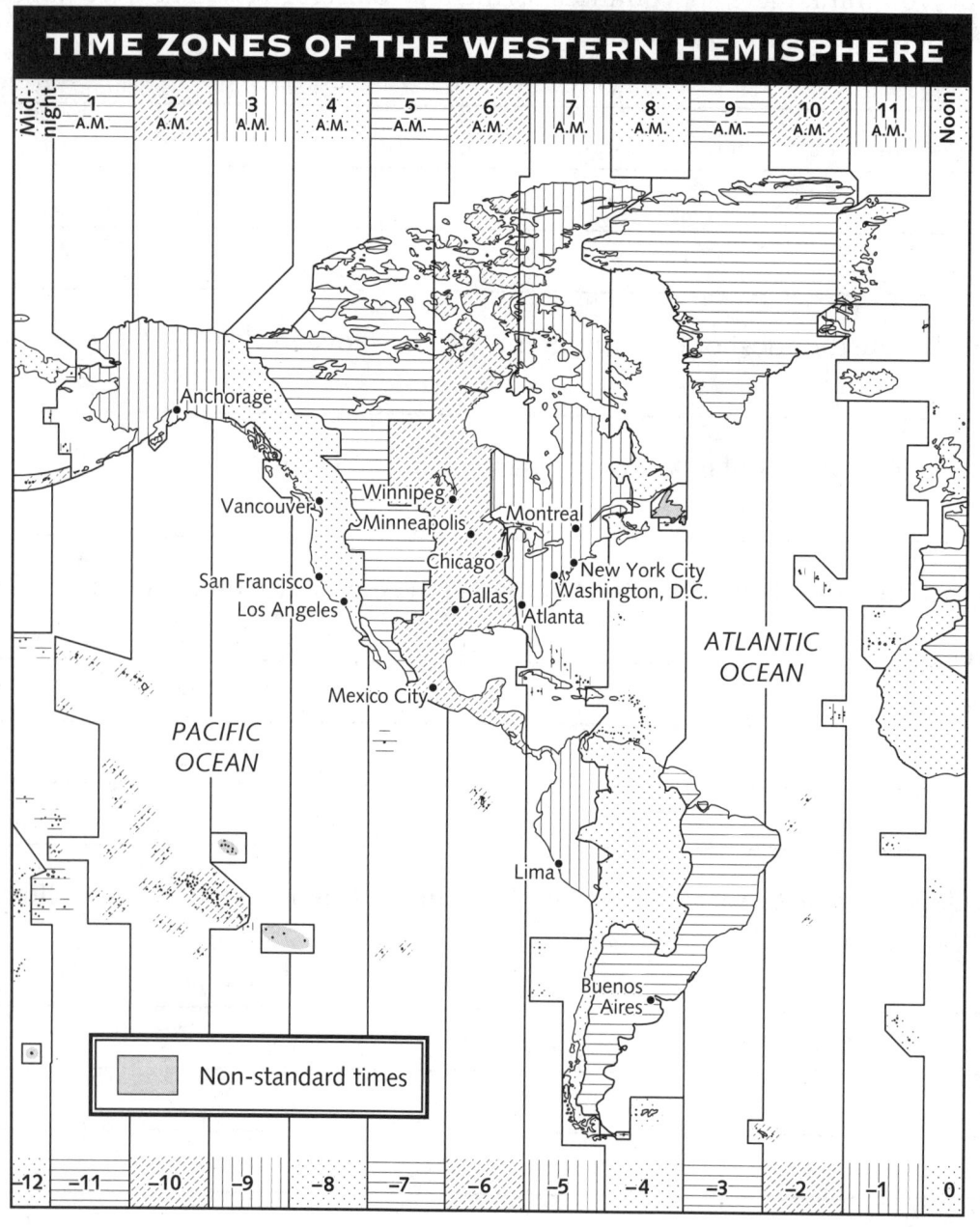

(Continued)

102 ACTIVITY BOOK

Use after reading Chapter 11, Skill Lesson, pages 462–463.

NAME _____   DATE _____

The U-Send-It message service of Los Angeles advertises that it will help people e-mail, fax, and place long-distance telephone calls to anyone, anywhere, anytime in the Western Hemisphere. The company's log for one day includes customer questions for you to answer. Use the map on page 102 to help you.

1. *6 A.M.* First customer from Los Angeles wants to know the answer to this question. If he faxes an important document right away, will it get to New York City in time for a noon meeting there? The answer and explanation are:

   Yes, when it is 6 A.M. in Los Angeles, it is only 9 A.M. in New York City; plenty of time for a

   fax to reach New York from Los Angeles.

2. *7 A.M.* Second customer wants to know when it is 3 A.M. in Anchorage, what time is it in Los Angeles. The answer is: 4 A.M.

3. *7:10 A.M.* Second customer asks another question, "When it is noon in San Francisco, what time is it in Washington, D.C.?" 3 P.M.

4. *9:05 A.M.* Third customer has an e-mail message to send and asks whether Chicago, Dallas, Lima, Mexico City, and Winnipeg are in same time zone. The answer is that all are in the Central time zone except for Lima.

5. *10:30 A.M.* Fourth customer from Los Angeles explains, "My cousin is expected back in Atlanta, Georgia, at 6 P.M. tonight. He promised to call to let me know when he gets home. What is the earliest time I can expect his message to arrive?"

   3 P.M. Los Angeles time

DIRECTIONS: Imagine that an international video conference is being set up among sixth-grade classes throughout the Western Hemisphere. When it is 10:20 A.M. in Minneapolis, what time is it in the three other cities listed below? Write the correct time for each city on the lines below.

Vancouver	Montreal	Minneapolis	Buenos Aires
8:20 A.M.	11:20 A.M.	10:20 A.M.	1:20 P.M.

Use after reading Chapter 11, Skill Lesson, pages 462–463.

NAME _____ DATE _____

The National Bamboo Project of Costa Rica

Draw Conclusions

DIRECTIONS: Read the paragraphs and answer the questions.

Bamboo, a giant grass, is helping to save the rain forests of Costa Rica. More than that, bamboo is providing low-cost housing for the poor, protecting river basins, and helping the environment by capturing and storing carbon dioxide from the atmosphere. Since 1986, the National Bamboo Project of Costa Rica has built hundreds of homes, provided work for unemployed people, and started new furniture and craft industries.

The project began with a search to find a substitute for wood that would be affordable and a good building material. Its many benefits include road repairs, a steadier supply of drinking water, and improvement of health conditions.

The project has been an international effort. The government of the Netherlands is helping to pay for it. The United Nations Development Program is helping to run it. The National Bamboo Project has been so successful that it is being used in other countries where bamboo can grow.

1. How might the National Bamboo Project protect rain forests from deforestation?

If bamboo is planted and harvested in place of trees, trees will not have to be cut down; bamboo can be used in place of wood for building homes; planting bamboo will protect river basins and will capture and store carbon dioxide.

2. In what ways does international cooperation help the National Bamboo Project?

When other countries cooperate with the National Bamboo Project, more bamboo will be planted around the world.

NAME _____ DATE _____

HOW TO READ AND COMPARE Climographs

Apply Chart and Graph Skills

DIRECTIONS: Using the information in the table below, complete the climograph that follows.

HONG KONG												
	JAN	FEB	MAR	APRIL	MAY	JUNE	JULY	AUG	SEP	OCT	NOV	DEC
Temperature	60	59	63	71	78	81	82	82	81	77	69	63
Precipitation	1.3	1.8	2.9	5.4	11.5	15.5	15.0	14.2	10.1	4.5	1.7	1.2

Temperatures are given in degrees (°) Fahrenheit. Precipitation information is given in inches.

DIRECTIONS: Compare the climograph of Hong Kong with the climograph of Tokyo on page 472 of your textbook. Then answer the questions that follow.

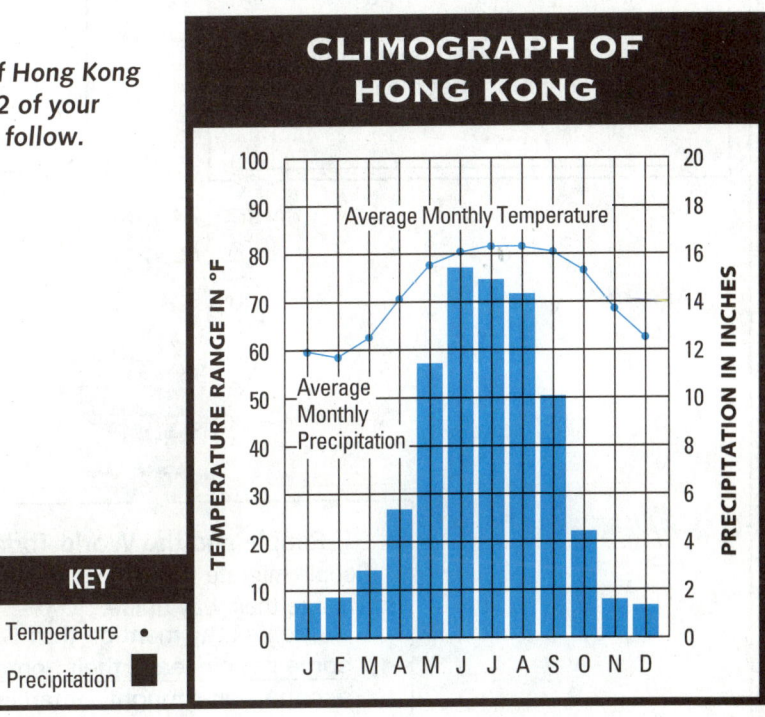

1. Which city is warmer in July? _Hong Kong_

2. Which city has the most rain in October? _Tokyo_

3. During which month of the year does Hong Kong receive the most rainfall?
June

Use after reading Chapter 11, Skill Lesson, pages 472–473.

NAME _____ DATE _____

PEOPLE AND PLACES

Connect Main Ideas

DIRECTIONS: Use this organizer to describe the countries and peoples of the world today and the challenges they face. Write two details to support each main idea.

Countries of the World Today
Both geography and history have helped form the countries of the world today.

1. Possible answers: history gave the Americas a diverse population; the fall of communism affected the size and existence of countries in Europe; the forming of countries in Asia was affected by religion and geography;
2. the borders of countries in Africa were formed based on natural resources; most people in Australia live along the coast

People and the Environment
People of the world today affect and are affected by their environments.

1. Students may mention that countries trade natural resources; that the environment keeps population from being spread evenly around the world; and that people change the environment positively and negatively to meet their needs.
2. _____

People and Places

People and the World Today
People migrate from one place to another to change their way of life.

1. Students may mention that some people leave their homes to escape war, drought, or famine; to gain political or religious freedom; or to find a better way of living in the cities.
2. _____

106 ACTIVITY BOOK — Use after reading Chapter 11, pages 444–477.

NAME _____ DATE _____

Milestones in Energy

Make Inferences from a Chart

DIRECTIONS: Since ancient times people have invented ways to make life easier and more productive. Nowhere is this shown more clearly than in the long history of using resources for energy. The chart below shows some early milestones in energy technology. Study the chart. Then answer the questions.

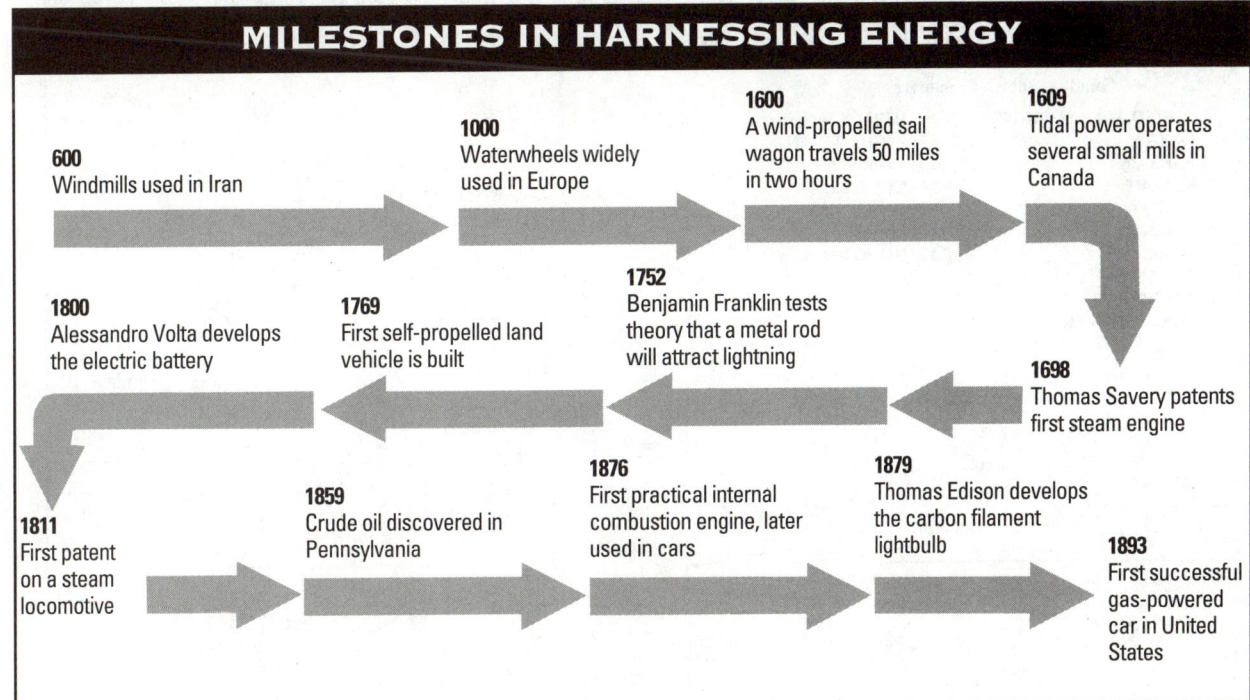

1. What important invention came at the end of the seventeenth century?
   the steam engine

2. Before the steam engine, what were some commonly used sources of power?
   water, wind, and tides

3. Did Benjamin Franklin use an electric battery in his experiments in 1752?
   no; because the battery was not invented until later

4. Do you think people in different countries would be wise to cooperate in the field of energy? Explain your answer.
   Students may answer that by sharing energy technology, countries may find new ways to control energy for the benefit of everyone; that countries who cooperate in the field of energy can help protect the energy resources that already exist.

Use after reading Chapter 12, Lesson 1, pages 479–487.

NAME _____ DATE _____

How to Read a Cartogram

CARTOGRAM OF ASIA IN 2010: PROJECTED POPULATION

Countries shown by number

1. UNITED ARAB EMIRATES
2. QATAR
3. BAHRAIN
4. KUWAIT
5. JORDAN
6. LEBANON
7. ISRAEL
8. ARMENIA
9. AZERBAIJAN
10. TURKMENISTAN
11. UZBEKISTAN
12. AFGHANISTAN
13. TAJIKISTAN
14. KYRGYZSTAN
15. CAMBODIA
16. MACAO
17. HONG KONG

(continued)

108   ACTIVITY BOOK

Use after reading Chapter 12, Skill Lesson, pages 488–489.

NAME _____ DATE _____

Apply Map and Globe Skills

DIRECTIONS: Review the cartogram on page 108. Then compare it with the political map of Asia and Europe on pages A8 and A9 of your textbook. Check the box before each statement below that applies to the cartogram or the political map. Some statements may apply to both.

CARTOGRAM	POLITICAL MAP	STATEMENT
	√	Shows countries in correct geographic location
	√	Identifies major bodies of water
√		Provides population information
	√	Shows exact location of countries
	√	Shows correct sizes of countries
	√	Shows correct shapes of countries
√	√	Shows all the countries of Asia

DIRECTIONS: Use either the cartogram on page 108 or the political map of Asia and Europe on pages A8 and A9 of your textbook to answer the questions below. In the space to the left of each question, write a C if you found the answer on the cartogram or a P if you found the answer on the political map.

1. __P__ What is the capital of Indonesia? __Jakarta__

2. __P__ What river system in Iraq empties into the Persian Gulf? __Tigris-Euphrates__

3. __C__ What country is expected to be the most populated country in Asia in 2010? __China__

4. __P__ Is Indonesia south or north of India? __south__

5. __P__ Describe the shape of Sri Lanka. __It is shaped like a teardrop.__

6. __C__ Will North Korea or South Korea have more people in 2010? __South Korea__

7. __P__ Which is the largest country in Asia? __China__

8. __P__ What body of water separates Japan from the mainland of Asia? __the Sea of Japan__

9. __C__ If about 100 million people will live in Iran in 2010, about how many people do you think will live in South Korea? __50 million__

Use after reading Chapter 12, Skill Lesson, pages 488–489.

NAME _____ DATE _____

The Conflict over Tibet

Read for Comprehension

DIRECTIONS: Read the paragraphs. Then answer the questions that follow.

Tibet is a land of unresolved conflict between native people and their rulers. Before 1950 Tibet was an independent country with ancient customs and a Buddhist religion. Today Tibet is part of China.

When Communist China captured Tibet in 1950, both sides agreed that Tibet would keep control over its religion and everyday life but China would have control over Tibet's international affairs. Soon China demanded more and more from Tibet. Conditions grew so tense that in 1959, the Dalai Lama, the spiritual ruler of Tibet, fled to India. In 1965, China took total control of Tibet. Since then Tibetans have taken their orders from Beijing, the distant Chinese capital. Hundreds of thousands of Chinese soldiers stationed in Tibet make sure those orders are obeyed.

Many Tibetans blame the Chinese for taking away their freedom, for harming their religious leaders, and for destroying their sacred temples. Their Chinese rulers disagree. The Chinese believe that they have helped the Tibetan people replace old-fashioned traditions with a better, modern way of life. Meanwhile, across the border in India, the Dalai Lama and many of his followers wait for the time when they can return to their homes in a free Tibet.

1. What is the main idea of the article about Tibet?
Once Tibet was an independent country, but it is now a part of China.

2. What reasons are there for the conflict between Tibet and China?
Tibetans blame China for taking away their freedom; the Chinese believe they are helping the people of Tibet.

NAME _____ DATE _____

HOW TO RESOLVE Conflict

Apply Critical Thinking Skills

DIRECTIONS: For each step below, write your arguments for or against a single government for all of Europe. You may need to write your answers outside the boxes or on a separate sheet of paper.

DECIDE WHAT YOU WANT TO ACHIEVE
Students should choose to work for or against a United States of Europe.

DECIDE WHAT YOU ARE WILLING TO GIVE UP
Students should list what they will give up to achieve their goal.

EXPRESS TO THE OTHER SIDE, EITHER ORALLY OR IN WRITING, WHAT YOU WANT AND LISTEN TO WHAT THEY WANT
Pair students—those who want to join with those who do not—to exchange papers.

EVALUATE THE OTHER SIDE'S RESPONSE AND FIND AREAS OF AGREEMENT AND COMPROMISE
The students in each pair should evaluate each other's reasons for and against a United States of Europe. Have students repeat the steps of the process to reach a compromise. After each pair has reached a compromise, have students share their findings on the process of compromise with the class.

Repeat the first four steps, if compromise is not reached.

Use after reading Chapter 12, Skill Lesson, pages 498–499.

ACTIVITY BOOK   111

NAME _____ DATE _____

DEMOCRACY,
British vs. American Style

Compare and Contrast Information

DIRECTIONS: The governments of the United States and Britain are democracies that serve as models for many other countries. Although both governments are similar in some ways, there are also many differences. Study the table. Then, on a separate sheet of paper, answer the question that follows.

	UNITED STATES	**BRITAIN**
Constitution	Written, originally, in 1787 and ratified in 1788	No separate document, constitution based on ordinary laws, some very old but many from the Reform Act of 1832
Monarchy	None	Appoints the prime minister and invites him or her to form a government by selecting a cabinet
Chief of State	President, elected in a national election	Prime minister, selected by his/her party's leaders, often in private
Separation of Powers	Clear separation between executive, legislative, and judicial branches of government, reinforced by many checks and balances	No separation between executive and legislative branches of government; Prime minister is a member of Parliament
Cabinet	Chosen by President with consent of Senate to serve as heads of executive departments; party membership is not required	Members must belong to the party that is in the majority in the House of Commons; all cabinet members are members of Parliament and take a lead in running it
Representative Bodies	Congress made up of the Senate and the House of Representatives	Parliament made up of House of Lords and House of Commons
Elections	Holds national, free elections, every 4 years for President, 2 years for representatives to Congress, and 6 years for Senators	House of Commons members chosen by national, free elections held at least every 5 years; but if prime minister loses vote of confidence in House, the prime minister can ask monarch to dissolve parliament and call for new elections
Political Parties	Two major political parties	Two major political parties

1. What do you think are the most important differences between the governments of the United States and Britain? The United States has a division between executive and legislative branches while Britain does not; Britain has a prime minister and a ceremonial monarch while the United States has a president.

NAME _____ DATE _____

HOW TO FORM A Logical Conclusion

Apply Critical Thinking Skills

DIRECTIONS: You have learned about the different kinds of governments. Match each quotation with the form of government the quotation represents. Read each quotation carefully for clues so that you can base your choice on a logical conclusion. Some forms of government are used more than once.

1. __D__ "My form of government rests in the choice of the people, by the people, and for the people."

2. __E__ "We have free elections for our country but the members of our Senate are appointed."

3. __F__ "There is only one party in my country, and everyone has to vote for the person that the party tells you to vote for."

4. __B__ "The queen is the head of my government, but her powers are very limited."

5. __G__ "In my country, power rests with groups of people, but they are all members of one political party."

6. __F__ "One day I decided to abolish the constitution and did so."

7. __A__ "A member of my family has ruled this country for hundreds of years. The people have no choice."

8. __B__ "We have a monarch, but it is the prime minister who really runs the country."

9. __C__ "The powers and requirements of our elected leaders are written in our constitution."

10. __F__ "I am the ruler of my country, and I control the lives of all my subjects."

A. absolute monarchy

B. constitutional monarchy

C. constitutional democracy

D. representative democracy

E. parliamentary democracy

F. dictatorship

G. oligarchy

Use after reading Chapter 12, Skill Lesson, page 507.

NAME _____ DATE _____

Looking at the Pacific Rim

Draw Conclusions from a Map

DIRECTIONS: Study the map. Then answer the questions.

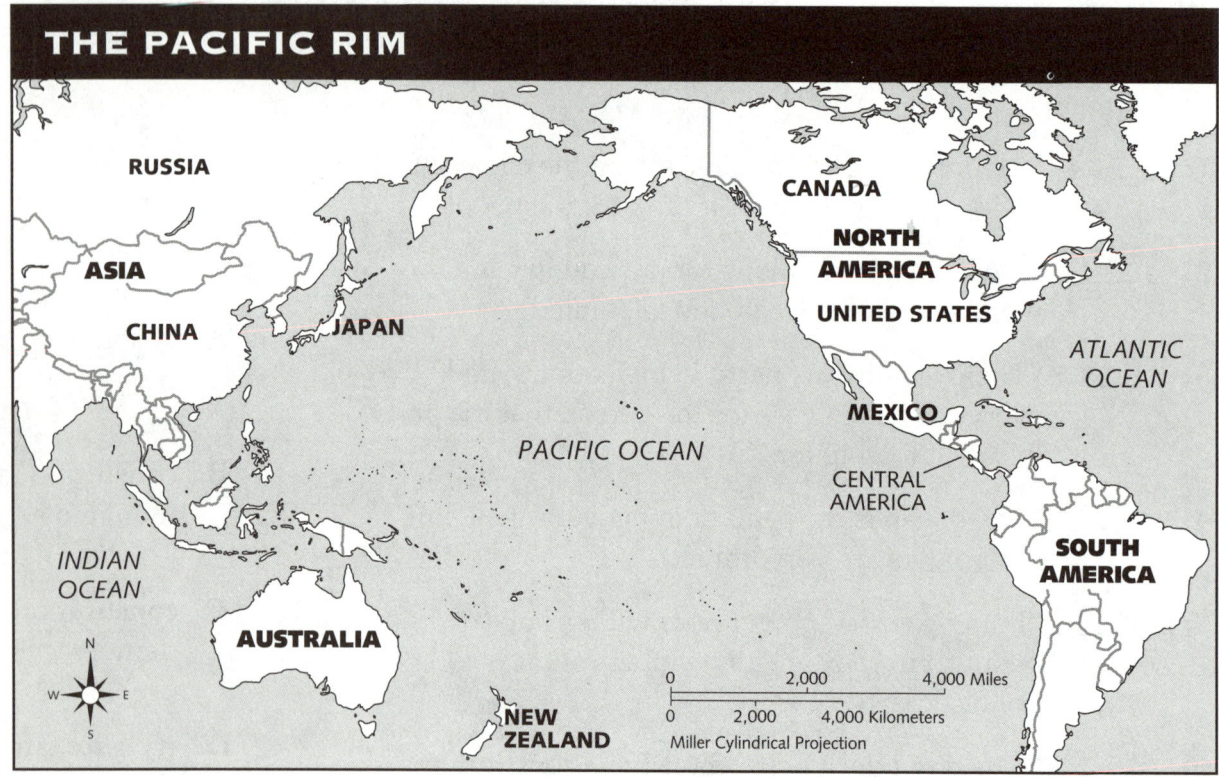

1. What do all the countries on this map have in common?
   They are located alongside the Pacific Ocean.

2. What do you think the term *Pacific Rim* means?
   Rim means "the outer border." The *Pacific Rim* refers to the outer border of the Pacific Ocean, where many countries lie.

3. Why do you think Pacific Rim countries might be likely to trade with one another?
   They have easy access to one another through the Pacific Ocean.

4. Think of the environment, trade, and cultural and information exchanges. On another sheet of paper, write a paragraph that tells how the different countries of the Pacific Rim might help one another in the next century.

114   ACTIVITY BOOK   Use after reading Chapter 12, Lesson 4, pages 508–513.

NAME _____ DATE _____

History, Government, and Economy

Connect Main Ideas

DIRECTIONS: Use this organizer to describe history, government, and economy in today's world. Write two details to support each main idea.

Events That Shaped the World
Contacts between cultures affected world history.

1. Students may mention that cultures came into contact through trade, the crusades, and war; that imperi-
2. alism and nationalism brought some countries together but also caused conflict.

Recent Events in the World
Conflicts have existed between countries of the world in recent years.

1. Students may mention the Berlin Wall, apartheid in Africa, the breakup of the Soviet Union, ethnic
2. cleansing in Bosnia, and the Arab-Israeli conflict.

Governments of the World Today
Different systems of government work in different ways.

1. Students may mention how democracy, monarchy, dictatorship, and ogliarchy work and what coun-
2. tries of the world use these different forms of government.

Working Together in Today's World
Countries form groups to work together.

1. Students may mention world trade and telecommunication as bringing countries together; and NAFTA,
2. OPEC, WTO, EU, and the UN as a few of the groups that have formed as a result.

(Center: History, Government, and Economy)

Use after reading Chapter 12, pages 478–515.

ACTIVITY BOOK 115